The Mental Athlete

Kay Porter, PhD

Porter Performance Systems
Eugene, OR

Human Kinetics

Library of Congress Cataloging-in-Publication Data

Porter, Kay.
    The mental athlete / Kay Porter.
        p. cm.
"A book by Kay Porter and Judy Foster with the same title was published by William C. Brown and Ballantine Books in 1986. This 2004 version of The mental athlete is a completely new book"--T.p. verso.
Includes bibliographical references and index.
    ISBN 0-7360-4654-2 (softcover)
    1.   Sports--Psychological aspects.   I. Title.
    GV706.4. P565 2003
    796' .01--dc21

2003007591

ISBN: 0-7360-4654-2

The Web addresses cited in this text were current as of May 2003, unless otherwise noted.

Developmental Editor: Laura Pulliam; **Assistant Editor:** Alisha Jeddeloh; **Copyeditor:** Patrick W. Connolly; **Proofreader:** Erin Cler; **Indexer:** Nancy Ball; **Permission Manager:** Toni Harte; **Graphic Designer:** Andrew Tietz; **Graphic Artist:** Tara Welsch; **Cover Designer:** Keith Blomberg; **Photographer (cover):** Dan Wendt; **Photographer (interior):** ©Human Kinetics unless otherwise noted; **Art and Photo Manager:** Dan Wendt; **Illustrator:** Dan Wendt; **Printer:** Transcontinental

Human Kinetics books are available at special discounts for bulk purchase. Special editions or book excerpts can also be created to specification. For details, contact the Special Sales Manager at Human Kinetics.

Printed in Canada   10   9   8   7   6   5   4   3   2   1

Human Kinetics
Web site: www.HumanKinetics.com

United States: Human Kinetics
P.O. Box 5076, Champaign, IL 61825-5076
800-747-4457
e-mail: humank@hkusa.com

Canada: Human Kinetics
475 Devonshire Road Unit 100
Windsor, ON N8Y 2L5
800-465-7301 (in Canada only)
e-mail: orders@hkcanada.com

Europe: Human Kinetics
107 Bradford Road, Stanningley
Leeds LS28 6AT, United Kingdom
+44 (0) 113 255 5665
e-mail: hk@hkeurope.com

Australia: Human Kinetics
57A Price Avenue
Lower Mitcham, South Australia 5062
08 8277 1555
e-mail: liahka@senet.com.au

New Zealand: Human Kinetics
P.O. Box 105-231, Auckland Central
09-523-3462
e-mail: hkp@ihug.co.nz

> "When I stepped on the ice, I had a feeling I knew what the Olympics were about. I had that feeling of just pure joy, and I went out there and put it in my program."
>
> Tara Lipinski, 15-year-old
> Olympic gold medalist in figure skating,
> 1998 Nagano Winter Games

Contents

Preface

As the title of this book suggests, *The Mental Athlete* is written for you, the athlete, and your team, whether you are an elite or recreational athlete. An early edition was in print for 12 years and was used by thousands of athletes and teams to help them prepare for competition and to overcome mental and psychological blocks to their peak performances. It helped them achieve their highest goals with mental fluidity and grace. As an athlete, if you want control over what your physical energy creates, you must maintain an awareness of your thoughts and intentions.

The philosophy behind this work is that for athletes to control and channel physical energy most effectively, they must be aware of their thoughts and intentions. Your thoughts are your reality. Your intentions are your goals—the reality you wish to achieve in your sport participation and your life. What are your goals? What are your intentions for the day, the week, the month, and the season?

Like most athletes, you've trained hard to overcome the physical barriers to peak performance in your sport. And yet you may not have paid the same attention or applied the same effort to the equally important mental and emotional factors influencing your performance.

How do you think? What are you thinking when you compete? How do you control your emotions when you are competing? How do you get into the "zone" associated with masterful performance? If you want to answer these questions, develop a mental mastery of your sport, and produce dominant performances in competition, this book is for you.

The Mental Athlete may represent the first step to mental consciousness for athletes. It teaches, sometimes for the first time, the idea that they *can* control their minds and their emotions, and that they can discipline their minds to imagine and create what they want to achieve in their lives. And that is a very powerful concept to recognize and master!

This book shows you the way to do that with the use of five simple tools. The early edition of *The Mental Athlete*, written in the mid-'80s, was a smashing success because it was simple, applied, and written from the heart. I have received hundreds of letters from readers sharing their excitement, joys, and successes . . . and their acknowledgment that they are in control of their minds and emotions in positive and productive ways—readers who are no longer being controlled by their negative thoughts and feelings, especially in intense competitive situations.

This book includes information on mental training, mental logs, goal setting, positive self-statements, relaxation, visualization, focusing, and concentration. It will help you to design your own program for peak performance, tell you how to get in the zone of peak performance, and explain how to deal with problems and blocks in competition.

This work also has special interest chapters on youth sports, health and healing, and psychological issues of the female athlete. It even has a chapter on mental training for peak performance in life so you can apply these concepts to your life outside sports. It is the only sport psychology book that will take you into the 21st century and beyond, helping you to achieve your peak potential in sports and in life.

It has always been important to me to practice the concepts that I discuss in my books and workshops. My learning in the last 20 years has been about simplicity, flexibility, setting my intention or goals, and learning to let go. Athletes who practice these skills become masters in their sports.

These issues are very significant for me because they represent issues that I work with daily in my personal and professional life. It is important to me personally to create a meaningful life for myself by balancing my work and play, having loving personal relationships, and living an ongoing healthy lifestyle of physical fitness and emotional and spiritual well-being. I strive to be the best I can be, to live my life with intensity and passion, and to give love and acceptance to myself and others.

I believe that in the new millennium, more and more athletes will begin to embrace the philosophy of expanding their minds and their conscious awareness. They will strive to become awake and aware and in tune with others on their teams and in their lives. My hope is that *The Mental Athlete* will foster this seed in all the athletes who read it.

I believe that more and more athletes and coaches are recognizing that they can go only so far on physical tools alone. My hope is that *The Mental Athlete* can serve as your primary training guide for expanding and strengthening your psychological prowess and emotional control to complement and enhance your physical abilities. And when you have the full package of physical, mental, and emotional skills, it then comes down to special attributes like heart and passion that only you can bring to the competitive arena.

Because it emphasizes vision, intention, purpose, and peak performance, mental skills training is the first essential step to creating a reality where you honor and accept yourself, thereby learning to honor and accept others as they are, not as you wish them to be. Thus, ultimately, with a fully prepared and activated mind, body, spirit, and heart, you can achieve peak performance.

Kay Porter, PhD
Porter Performance Systems
P.O. Box 5584
Eugene, Oregon 97405
541-342-6875
KayPorter1@aol.com
www.thementalathlete.com

Acknowledgments

I would like to thank...

Judy Foster-Filppi, who co-wrote the best-selling early edition of *The Mental Athlete* with me. Without her friendship, help, and support, this would not have been possible. I am grateful for her friendship, her creativity, and her heart-centered energy.

The University of Oregon athletic department and coaching staff, who were open and trusting enough in the early days of our work to let Judy and me work with their athletes and teams.

Joe Henderson, West Coast editor of *Runner's World* and a longtime friend, for his inspiration, modeling, and mentorship, and for believing in me and my work long before it was popularly accepted.

Joan Ullyot, whose book, *Women's Running*, and friendship inspired me to train for and run seven marathons.

Tom Jordan, co-director of the Prefontaine Classic Grand Prix track-and-field meet, who gave me my first assignment and who allows me to interview the world-class track-and-field athletes who come to Eugene to compete.

The U.S. Olympic Committee sport psychology staff who support all of us on the USOC Sport Psychology Registry. Without their continued help and support, the Olympic teams and developmental programs would still be in their infancy. They have done a fantastic job of bringing the ideas and practices of mental training to the forefront of athletes' consciousness.

The athletes—the beginners, the weekend warriors, the young and aspiring, the elite, and the coaches. With your combined wisdom, inspiration, and support, this training evolved and matured. Thank you all!

> **Man is what he believes.**
> Anton Chekhov

Chapter 1

Essentials for Effective Mental Training

The purpose of life is to grow.

What do Marion Jones, Michael Jordan, and Tiger Woods have in common? Between them they have won assorted Olympic medals, world championship rings, and large trophies. More important, all three of them possess tremendous mental skills that enhance their athletic performance and put them at the top of their respective sports. This book defines a program of mental training that will help you develop your own mental skills. If used with dedication and discipline, this program will help you reach your peak athletic performance.

Mental training focuses on the positive aspects of an athlete's mental performances, physical abilities, and preparation skills. The program in this book will help you identify what is already working for you. It will also teach you how to expand what is working in order to improve your performance. Using mental training strategies, you can gain more control over what happens during important competitions by being completely prepared in mind, body, and spirit.

This mental training program is based on the idea that the pictures in your mind have real power; you create your own reality with your mental images—how you "see" yourself and your abilities, whether positively or negatively. These images affect your performance now and in the future. For example, if you see yourself as a slow and awkward person, you will manifest these traits in athletic events. On the other hand, if you learn to see yourself as a winner and a competent athlete, this too will manifest itself in your performance.

Current research indicates that the pictures in the mind, also called visualizations, determine the atmosphere of a person's world. You create either positive or negative images for yourself as a person and as an athlete. Creating these images puts forth an intent of what will happen to you. Think for a minute about the last time you were around someone who was angry. You could feel their negative energy from across the room. Think now of the last time you were with someone who was excited, happy, and full of energy. Remember how their energy made you feel and how it affected your attitude and responses. If you go into an athletic competition feeling scared, uptight, and unsure of yourself, your teammates or competitors will feel this negative energy, and the negative energy will show in your performance. If you feel calm and confident, you create a positive atmosphere. By expecting the best, you put forth a positive intent that good things will happen, that you will succeed.

People who create positive intent become dreamers. They daydream about what they want and what they believe is possible—or maybe even impossible. These people imagine the difference that achieving a particular goal will make in their life, their work, and their athletic pursuits. They dream the impossible dream, and by dreaming it, they make it possible.

So, what's involved in mental training to achieve peak athletic performance? In this program, you will learn, practice, and apply mental skills through

- setting short- and long-term goals,
- changing negative thought patterns and perceptions into positive thought patterns and belief systems (reframing),
- writing positive self-statements (affirmations) about and in support of your athletic performance,
- performing progressive relaxation techniques,
- using visualization and imagery of your sport,
- concentrating and focusing, and
- coping mentally with injury and pain.

You should think of this mental training program in the same way as you think of your physical training program—for it to work best, you must practice it often. The program requires discipline and complete dedication to your athletic goals and dreams.

Some elite athletes seem to intuitively set up their own individual mental training program, and these athletes may believe they don't need a comprehensive program. However, many groups of athletes can benefit from this program. Among these are the following:

- Talented athletes who have yet to achieve their potential
- Athletes who need to learn to be more aggressive and competitive
- Elite athletes who are injured
- Elite athletes who want to improve their concentration
- All people who participate in sports and want to improve and to reach their peak performance

Embodying the Essentials

The idea of mental training, and sport psychology in general, draws many different responses from athletes, from "Hey, don't fool around with my head!" to "Sounds great!" to "It's worth a try to see what I can learn." Many coaches and athletes maintain that the ability to reach peak performance is 90 percent mental. It follows that all athletes, from the average to the elite, can learn by using this simple program and practicing mental skills as diligently as they practice their sports. Before you begin a mental training program, you must be willing to adopt a positive attitude in the following areas.

Being Ready to Change

If you are not willing to change, you will stay stuck in the same old patterns that are not working for you. A mental training program requires you to be more open mentally and emotionally to your own processes—how you play, how you think, and how you react, both positively and negatively, when you make mistakes. How do you recover from and let go of mistakes while moving forward and staying in the moment of the competition? Here are four tips for athletes who want to change behavior:

1. Make change a *priority*. Think about being mentally open and focus on making goals about paying attention.
2. Be willing to take *risks*. Do something new and let go of worries about looking or feeling stupid.

3. Make a personal *commitment*. Begin to make mental training goals that will help your performance.

4. Take *action*. Write these ideas down and really think about what you are doing mentally when you play and practice.

These four tips will help you move toward your goals for improving your mental edge.

Assuming Responsibility

As an athlete, how often have you blamed others for a loss? How often have you blamed yourself for your poor performance or placed the entire blame on yourself for the loss of a game? Is this attitude positive and does it work for you, or does it help to keep you stuck at your present performance level? Do you learn from your setbacks or do you look to assign blame for them? The bottom line is that you, and you alone, are responsible for the level of your performance. You may not be responsible if a fan throws a tin can that hits you in the head, but you are responsible for your reaction. You are responsible for your level of readiness and for your positive or negative frame of mind as you prepare to perform. You can choose to learn from a less-than-perfect performance and go forward using it to your advantage, or you can choose to become upset and tense and be defeated by your attitude. You are totally free to see yourself as important, competent, talented, and unique. You are also free to see yourself as incompetent, unworthy, untalented, and second best.

These choices are colored and dictated by your self-concept and personal support. Accepting responsibility for these choices often takes maturity and trust—trust in the process of living, trust in yourself as a competent athlete and person, and trust in your gut feeling. Take a moment to think about your own level of trust. What do you trust most about your athletic performance? What do you trust least about your performance? What do you think your coach or teammates trust most about you? What do they trust least about you? You may want to write these thoughts down to clarify your level of self-trust and to discover areas for improvement.

Making choices and creating inner trust are easier if you feel directed—if you have goals and the desire to head toward them, and if you are willing to be accountable for your choices and their consequences. With this newly found responsibility, you must reassess the way you approach competition and life.

Do you view competition and important workouts as threatening? Challenging? Or do you enter them for the love of the game? Think of the last athletic event you participated in that meant a lot to you. When the big play came to you, or when the outcome depended totally on you, did you pull it off or did you lose your concentration and choke? If you did succeed, what was your feeling? Relief? Joy? Elation? If you did not succeed, were you filled with anger and self-hatred for days or weeks? Or did you feel disappointed and dissatisfied for a few hours and then go on with life? If you enter competition feeling threatened, when you win, you only experience relief; when you lose, you blame and hate yourself or others for months or even years. If you view competition as a challenge,

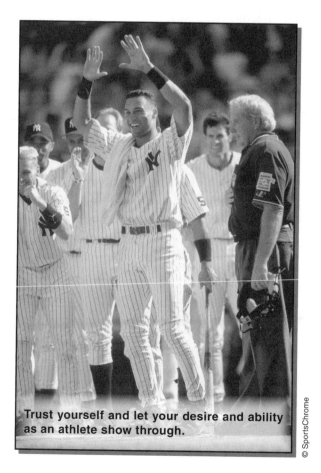

Trust yourself and let your desire and ability as an athlete show through.

© SportsChrome

you experience joy when you win and strong anger when you lose. Challenge often works as a strong motivator and can be a fairly successful strategy for many athletes. If you participate simply for the love of the game, you savor victory. You feel ecstasy and great enthusiasm when you win. And when you lose, you may be disappointed, but you learn from your mistakes and realize that you are not a loser—you have merely lost and will win again. The loss does not destroy your self-image, your self-esteem, or your belief in your abilities.

The motivation for the most successful athletes often falls between challenge and love of the game. They love their sport, have fun doing it, and are spurred by challenge. They understand that the attitude they bring to their performance is their choice and that it will either help them win or defeat them.

If you take the time to prepare mentally for your performance (realizing this preparation is fully your choice), form your goals, and feel directed and in control, many times you will succeed far beyond your expectations. You will win, if only within yourself, and you will experience the feeling of accomplishment that accompanies your peak performance.

Believing in Yourself

You are not your programming, your ego, or your personal past. You are not your acts, and you are not your successes or your failures. Then what *are* you? You are no more and no less than what you *think* you are. If you see yourself as a loser, as a victim, you will surely make yourself so. If you believe you are competent, powerful, and a winner, this is your reality. Your beliefs become self-perpetuating and self-confirming. How you think and what you believe determine your experience by confirming your self-concepts and creating your reality. You can change these belief patterns so that they work for you and change your reality to a positive and supportive system. It takes time, but it is possible. It means becoming aware of which beliefs limit you and taking a risk by changing what may be a lifelong habit. For example, here are some common beliefs that limit many athletes in their sports and in their lives:

- I have to earn respect.
- I must compete to please my dad.
- I have to earn love.

- No pain, no gain.
- It's not okay to have fun.
- It's not feminine for a woman to be an outstanding athlete.
- It's selfish to take time for myself and my training.
- I'm too slow, too dumb, too fat, too tall, too short, and so forth.
- It's not feminine for a girl to beat the boys.
- Being an outstanding athlete makes me acceptable to my peers.

Mental Trainer #1 will help you clarify a few of the beliefs that limit you. Take a few minutes to fill out the worksheet on page 8, or write down the information in a mental training notebook.

Training Yourself

This book is about finding your mental awareness, noticing what you do with it, and learning to make it work for you in every aspect of your life. To grow and learn in both athletics and in life, you must be willing to do the following:

- Take risks.
- Feel what's going on for you, especially in competition.
- Be in the present moment and let go of the past.
- Breathe when you are tense or scared.
- Have fun and enjoy yourself.
- Trust yourself and the process.
- Participate 100 percent without fear of failure.

Winning is as difficult or as easy as you make it. The choice is yours. When I interviewed Judi Brown King, an Olympic silver medalist in the 400-meter hurdles, she described the importance of mental training and its impact on her performance:

> Since I started running, I've always considered myself a mental runner. If I didn't believe I could do it, I wouldn't have a good race. You're describing me when you say "mental training." I started doing mental training when I first began running, but I started doing the mental preparation before I realized what I was doing. Especially the night before, I would break every world record there was in my

Mental Trainer #1: Beyond Your Limits

List a few of your beliefs that you feel limit your athletic performance. Think about this. For many people, it is extremely difficult to "see" their habits, to truly see what it is that may be holding them back.

My limiting beliefs are:

These limiting beliefs keep you stuck in the mud of your mind; they take away your power and feelings of competence and confidence. "Power" refers to a feeling of competency and well-being, not brute strength. It is a feeling generated by your inner voice and mind, a true sense of knowing. Go inside yourself for a moment and ask yourself these questions:

How do I feel when I feel powerless?

How do I feel when I am in my power, when I feel powerful?

What do I do to be in my power, to feel powerful?

How does it feel, sound, and look when I am in my power?

Listen to yourself as you continue these awareness questions. Be in touch with how connected or disconnected you are at this point with your personal mental process and how it guides your experience and reality.

Three ways I strip myself of my power in my sport are:

Three things I do to help myself keep my power in my sport are:

The most significant mental change I could make to reach a higher level of athletic performance would be:

images. The early morning, before I run, is when I really get into mental preparations. I imagine every single thing that could happen to alter the race—it's windy, it's raining, I hit the hurdle, I feel the "hump" between hurdle five and seven. That's the hump for me, the most difficult part of the race, and I know the feeling, so in the race I am ready for it. I've mentally prepared myself for it and I know how to react to it appropriately.

For instance, I tell myself, "So-and-so in the race got an excellent start . . . don't panic . . . ," and I adjust to that situation. I more or less know all the runners in the race and how they run so my images are very accurate. I've always been that way in life, preparing myself for any outcome. In all my tests through school, I'd figure out what the teacher stressed as important and learn that. I found myself to be very perceptive as to what someone perceived to be important.

When I start visualizing a race, the first thing I feel is that adrenaline surge. If you were to hook my heart up to an EKG and I started visualizing, my heart rate would probably go from low to a very high rate. I can imagine and visualize everything, even with my eyes open. [The] five minutes before a race is a runner's nightmare. Anything can happen. No matter how physically and mentally prepared you are, you can totally lose everything in the last five minutes. If you are distracted, you have to be able to pull yourself back on track mentally and refocus and concentrate. Even being strong-minded, you have to be able to turn negative situations into positives. The mental games runners play are amazing. For instance, when I started racing, one runner whose times were slightly better than mine came over before a race and sat directly in front of me so I could see her. Her "game" was to get me to focus on her instead of preparing myself for the race. It takes a strong mind to shut out a predicament such as that and still be successful.

As I mentioned before, in the last five minutes before the race, I prepare myself. When the official says, "Runners, take your mark," I think about driving out of the blocks, getting out well, because if I have an excellent first hurdle, I'm going to have an excellent race. If I have just a good start, I'll have a good race. Likewise if I have a bad start, I'll have a race of adjustments. The main thing I think about is, *Get out . . . get out!* Then when the starter says, "Set," I just think about the gun and wait for the sound to react to.

Even my negative experiences have become positive in the long run. I'm basically a positive-thinking person. In the difficult parts of my race, I [mentally] turn the pain threshold off. I concentrate on the mechanics of movement. I'm thinking about snapping the lead leg down instead of thinking, *I'm tired,* or possibly, *I'm behind.* I concentrate on staying relaxed by saying, "Stay relaxed." If I hit a hurdle, I say, "It's okay . . . let's make up the momentum you have lost." I tell myself, "Okay, you're still in good shape, up with the top three runners, let's try to get up in second or first so there are no more mishaps." Things like that. I give myself continuous pep talks.

One of Judi's most telling statements is, "[The] five minutes before a race is a runner's nightmare." And indeed, it can be for the athlete whose emotions are out of control and whose self-talk is negative. For an athlete who has practiced mental control, the final minutes before a race can be a time of solidity, mental toughness, and centeredness. The daily practice of mental training techniques can turn those five minutes into a pleasant interlude, a precursor to fulfilling a lifetime dream and goal.

The last 100 or 200 meters of a race again calls for mental tenacity. Judy described what she was thinking during the last 100 meters of the Olympic finals:

I was telling myself, "I've worked hard for this. Listen, I've given up too much to give up here! At least try for a medal!" I was running for my sacrifices. I began catching people. The gold medalist was too far ahead to catch. I ran negative splits [running the second half of the race faster than the first]. All in all, I was satisfied.

If I get down, distracted, or whatever, I make a decision to just turn it off. I don't let myself dwell on a situation or let it get to me. I didn't enjoy the Olympics too much. I had bad starts; I got lane eight when I should have had lane six, but somehow it wasn't given to me. I just put these situations on the shelf and turned it off mentally. I wouldn't let any bad breaks get to me.

It is this style of conscious decision making that athletes can learn to use. It can become a habit like anything else. This strategy can help athletes focus on their event and block out everything else. The mental state is one of acceptance, letting go, and returning internal focus to the event. Judi Brown King is an excellent role model in terms of attitude and mental preparation, and athletically, she is certainly a positive role model. She is a smooth and rhythmic runner who displays beauty and grace going over the hurdles. Even in practice doing her drills, she has style and grace. Her inner strength and peace are reflected both in her attitude and in her athletic performance: "I am basically a positive person and turn negative things around into a positive situation for me. I refuse to let things get me down."

Remember, a mental training program is an educational process, one that can help an athlete approach competition or an average person approach life with a more positive and enthusiastic frame of mind. The purpose of this book is to make you aware of your mental processes so that you can choose to change them if they are not working for you. The techniques in this book are your tools for discovery.

Chapter 2

Developing Mental Training Skills

For this is the great secret, which was known to all educated men in our day: we create the world around us, daily new . . .

M.Z. Bradley

The mental side of athletics is an exciting new area, and athletes are enjoying it. This area is something new and different, something to be explored, and athletes can see and feel it working. In the early 1980s, sport psychologists spent hours explaining the importance of mental training techniques to athletes and teams, and in the 1990s, great strides were made in the overall acceptance of these techniques. Today, sports commentators talk constantly about the use of sport psychology among elite athletes. With each passing year, there is more talk about how athletes work on their mental edge and what athletes do to prepare mentally.

Athletes are now ready for new ideas that will help them to be the best they can be. They are no longer worried about being seen as a "head case" if they work with a sport psychologist. Athletes know that, in addition to being physically fit and ready, they can perform even better by using their positive mental skills.

Improving Your Competitive Edge

These days, athletes are hungry for knowledge about how to improve their competitive, or winning, edge. Many athletes have begun to examine the spiritual part of competition because they know that the sharpest edge is mental. Phil Jackson is the former coach of the NBA champion Chicago Bulls. In his book, *Sacred*

Hoops: Spiritual Lessons of a Hardwood Warrior (1995), Jackson notes the following:

> In basketball—as in life—true joy comes from being fully present in each and every moment, not just when things are going your way. Of course, it's no accident that things are more likely to go your way when you stop worrying about whether you're going to win or lose and focus your full attention on what's happening *right this moment.*

Jackson's book has many examples of Eastern philosophies and Native American concepts being applied to sports. Currently, there is a lot of interest in Native American teachings, and in spiritual development and learning, and many more athletes in the 21st century will no doubt reach new spiritual levels through their sport achievements. The balance of mind, body, spirit, and emotions is part of the foundation of the Mental Athlete philosophy. In this philosophy, spirit is seen as joy and harmony within (not in a religious context, although some athletes may go that route).

In working with the Bulls, Jackson found that it was very effective to use the players' desire to connect with something larger than themselves. The team came first and what was good for the team was good for the players. Jackson views this as a spiritual process, even for players who don't see themselves as spiritual. The whole idea is for the individual players to let go of their self-interest for the greater good so that the team can win and be successful. Even the great Michael Jordan was able to put the team first, rather than being the "star," and in being a team player, he was a star anyway. It isn't easy to do this, especially in professional sports where young people are paid enormous amounts of money. Their egos often get in the way. But when players use all their mental, physical, and spiritual resources, magic often occurs. Mindfulness, the act of paying attention to the moment, creates this magic, and individuals become one with each other. Jackson describes this in his book:

> No team understood better than the championship Chicago Bulls that selflessness is the soul of teamwork. The conventional wisdom is that the team was primarily a one-man show—Michael Jordan, and the Jordanaires. But the real reason the Bulls won three straight NBA championships from 1991 to '93 was that we plugged in to the power of *oneness* instead of the power of one man, and transcended the divisive forces of the ego that have crippled far more gifted teams. (1995)

Achieving the Mental Edge

When two athletes of equal—and often unequal—ability compete, the athlete with the mental edge most often emerges as the winner. The good news is that you can achieve this edge with the use of five simple tools:

1. Mental log keeping
2. Effective goal setting
3. Positive self-talk or affirmations
4. Relaxation techniques
5. Visualization or imagery

Once you master these tools, you must remember that mental training requires you to make a commitment to be as dedicated to training your mind as you are to training your body. Daily mental practice prepares you for all possibilities and helps you cope positively with the unexpected, rather than becoming "psyched out."

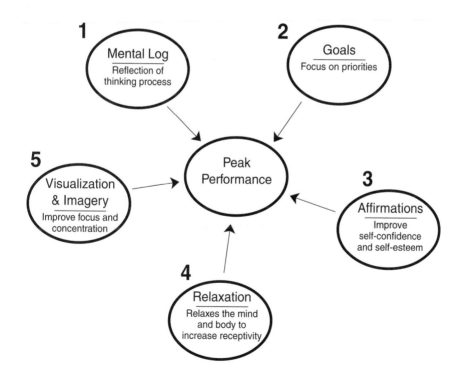

Using the five tools, you can create a positive mental state before, during, and after competition. By using mental training strategies, you create more personal control over what happens in competition. You are ready physically, and you are also mentally tough and ready—completely prepared in mind, body, and spirit.

The following chapters describe a program that enables you to achieve your peak performance by using the five mental training tools. Instructions for using these tools, along with many different examples, are interwoven throughout the book. Each chapter will provide information that helps you develop your skills at using one or more of the tools. When you have finished this book, you will be able to apply each tool to your own experiences, and you will have developed your own program for peak performance.

Mental training skills may be simple, but they are extremely powerful. When you set your goals, what you say to yourself and what you see and don't see are vitally important to your success.

Gail Devers, longtime hurdler champion, has superb focus and concentration skills.

© Empics

In the 21st century, teamwork is also emerging as an important aspect of sport peak performance. Phil Jackson's "The power of We is stronger than the power of Me" approach is important for athletes to remember. Both in sports and in business, team building and teamwork are increasingly important for success.

As an athlete, you must also look for the "path of the heart." Phil Jackson says it well:

> Obviously, there's an intellectual component to playing basketball. Strategy is important. But once you've done the mental work, there comes a point when you have to throw yourself into the action and put your heart on the line. That means not only being brave, but also being compassionate, toward yourself, your teammates, and your opponents. This idea was an important building block of my philosophy as a coach. More than anything else, what allowed the Bulls to sustain a high level of excellence was the players' compassion for each other. (1995)

From the great success of the Lakers under Phil Jackson's tutelage, it's clear he has taken that philosophy with him to Los Angeles.

Chapter 3

Gauging Your Mental Aptitude

Running is 80% mental.

Joan Benoit Samuelson

You must already be interested in how you can become mentally prepared for your sport or else you wouldn't have picked up this book. In the next few chapters, you will find ways to more easily identify your mental training goals and learn the steps in achieving those goals. You will learn to visualize and imagine your peak performance, and you will also learn how to change the negative self-talk and beliefs that are holding you back from performing at your best.

In this chapter, you will complete two self-tests to clarify your mental aptitude and attitude. These exercises will help you think about how you would improve each aspect of your mental ability.

Measuring Your Aptitude

The first two self-tests (see pages 21 and 22) are taken from the book *Sports Talent* (Brown 2001). These tests are easy to use, short, and to the point. Use these tests to evaluate your emotional talent and mental skills. On the Emotional Talent Checklist, circle the number that represents where you rate your current level of emotional aptitude for each item. If you give yourself a low score on a particular item, write down an action plan to help you focus on what to do about it. Write one or two concrete actions that you can take to improve your score on that item. For example, if you scored low on passion, your action plan might be to have more fun while you are playing or practicing.

But how would you do that, you ask? Perhaps by focusing on giving 110 percent while you are playing or practicing, or focusing on encouraging your teammates if you are playing a team sport. If you scored low on stability, which means handling stress or being resilient, an action plan might include remembering to keep breathing if you are nervous, or talking to yourself internally, encouraging yourself and telling yourself, "I am calm and focused. I let go of any mistakes easily." (You'll learn more about positive self-talk in chapter 4.)

The instructions for filling out the Mental Skills Evaluation are essentially the same as for the Emotional Talent Checklist (circle the number that best represents your current level of mental skill for each item). This evaluation, though, is designed so that it can also be used in a team environment. Each member of the team should fill out the evaluation and then choose a partner. Partners can then compare scores and help each other find ways to improve each skill. Again, turn suggestions into action plans so that you can improve your mental performance.

Many questions about how to improve these skills will be answered in later chapters of this book. For some athletes, mental skills and ability are innate. They seem to be born with drive, passion, and mental toughness. The good news for others is that these mental skills can be learned with application, diligence, and the will to change. You too can become a mentally tough competitor and have the mental edge that so many others enjoy. What you focus on and work on, you can create. So be patient with yourself and trust the process of your learning.

Putting Your Results in Perspective

After taking these tests, you may feel overwhelmed by how many things you want to change. Make a list of the items where you scored 3 or below (see page 24). Then pick one or two items to work on each week. In a short time, you'll improve many of your mental attitudes about competitions or practices. After practicing each mental skill for a week, they will start to become positive habits. Take one or both of these self-tests every three months to check on your progress and to keep yourself focused on improving. You'll be amazed how quickly your mental skills improve.

Your body is strengthened if you put in your physical training on the field, on the court, or in the weight room. Similarly, if you practice your mental skills on a daily basis, your mental toughness and mental abilities will be strengthened. In a few short weeks, you can build yourself into a strong, mentally tough performer.

Emotional Talent Checklist

- Circle the number that applies to you (1 is low; 5 is high).
- Determine one action to address weakest areas.
- Discuss with a friend, parent, coach, or sport psychologist.

1. **Drive** (overwhelming desire to succeed)   1 2 3 4 5
   Action plan:

2. **Passion** (loves the game; can't stay away from it)   1 2 3 4 5
   Action plan:

3. **Stability** (can handle stress; resilient)   1 2 3 4 5
   Action plan:

4. **Toughness** (good self-esteem; confident)   1 2 3 4 5
   Action plan:

5. **Positive Attitude** (enjoys challenges;
   avoids negative thinking)   1 2 3 4 5
   Action plan:

6. **Realism** (works on limitations; learns from experience) 1 2 3 4 5
   Action plan:

7. **Focus** (blocks out distractions; absorbed in the game) 1 2 3 4 5
   Action plan:

8. **Effort** (first on and off the field or court;
   keeps improving)   1 2 3 4 5
   Action plan:

9. **Persistence** (can manage desire to be perfect)   1 2 3 4 5
   Action plan:

10. **Competitiveness** (refuses to lose; likes the battle)   1 2 3 4 5
    Action plan:

Adapted, by permission, from Jim Brown, 2001, *Sports talent* (Champaign, IL: Human Kinetics), 38.

Mental Skills Evaluation

Name:

Event:

Circle a number for each item (1 is low; 5 is high).

1. **Mental preparation prior to game**   1 2 3 4 5
   How can I improve this?

2. **Precompetition activity**   1 2 3 4 5
   How can I get ready?

3. **Emotional readiness**   1 2 3 4 5
   How can I be emotionally ready?

4. **Self-confidence**   1 2 3 4 5
   How can I increase my self-confidence?

5. **Quality of effort**   1 2 3 4 5
   How can I improve my quality of effort?

6. **Concentration**   1 2 3 4 5
   How can I improve my concentration?

7. **Consistency of focus**   1 2 3 4 5
   How can I focus better and more consistently?

8. **Mental toughness**   1 2 3 4 5
   How can I be more mentally tough?

9. **Ability to let go of mistakes**   1 2 3 4 5
   How can I let go of mistakes easily?

10. **Poise**   1 2 3 4 5
    How can I be more poised?

11. **Control of negative thoughts**   1 2 3 4 5
    How can I control my negative thinking?

12. **Enjoyment**   1 2 3 4 5
    How can I have more fun?

13. **Communication with teammates**   1 2 3 4 5
    How can I communicate better with my teammates?

What aspects of your competition in today's event were you pleased with?

What aspects of your competition in today's event were you disappointed with?

Adapted, by permission, from Jim Brown, 1993, *Penn State Sports Medicine Newsletter* 7(7):3.

Mental Toughness Attributes

Items where I scored 3 or below :

1.

2.

3.

4.

5.

6.

7.

8.

9.

10.

Chapter 4

Taking Steps Toward Positive Thinking

If you continue to do what you have always done, you will continue to get what you have always gotten.

Gary Koyen

Of the five mental training tools, the first three (mental log keeping, effective goal setting, and positive self-talk or affirmations) are included in this chapter. This chapter leads you through a step-by-step process that uses these three tools to help you build a positive mental attitude. To set meaningful goals for yourself, you must first keep a mental training log. This log will help you identify how you think, both positively and negatively, and what you want to change in your thinking habits. From the information in the log, you can write meaningful physical and mental goals for yourself. After you write your goals, you can then turn them into sentences or affirmations that will help you to maintain a positive attitude.

Logging Your Thoughts

Just as you keep track of your physical training and conditioning, so should you keep track of your mental training. You have thought processes that benefit and support you in a multitude of ways, and you also have beliefs and habits that tend to limit you. Most of the time you are not aware of what these are or of how they help or hinder you.

Keeping a written log to monitor and analyze your thoughts and responses to competition helps you become more aware of your mental process. As you progress, you will eventually have more control over your patterns of thought and your beliefs, and therefore more control over your performance.

A mental training log (see page 27) is a diary that you write in after each significant workout, event, or competition. It is a written account of your emotional and intellectual process as you warm up, perform, and conclude your physical activity. It contains your inner thoughts and pictures, your fears, and your emotional strengths. Your mental training log tells the story of how you as an athlete, and ultimately a person, think, react, process, and support your physical performance and competence. Your log is also a place to write down all the anger, frustration, and negativity you might feel after a poor performance. You can use the log as a starting point for a new attitude, a way of letting go of your frustration, self-doubt, and blame so that you can start building a more positive and confident mental attitude. Your mental training log will help you use your performance as a learning experience—your first step toward excellence.

Here's an example of how it works. You are a figure skater entering your first competition of the year. You are not too sure of the ice or the judges, and you have not competed since last winter. You also know that last year's state champion is competing just after you. You stand at the edge, waiting to hear your name, waiting to step onto the ice. What is happening in your head? Are you breathing? Is your coach talking to you, giving you some last-minute instructions? Do you hear the words? How do they make you feel?

As you step down and begin to glide across the ice, how does your body feel in general? Are you relaxed and smooth, or are you tense and stiff? What is your reaction to your physical state of being? If you fall, what do you say to yourself? If you do your triple Axel perfectly, what is your inner voice saying? While you are competing, focus on your performance. When you finish, become aware as much as possible of the inner words, concepts, and feelings that guided you to do well or to do less than your best.

Within 24 hours, write down this mental awareness in a mental training log. Write it down fully, from beginning to end, good and bad. Be as clear and honest as you can, noting as many internal words and beliefs as you remember. You may remember that when you stepped onto the ice you were thinking, *Well, here we go . . . let's have fun . . . you know you're ready*. You may remember that when you saw the state champion standing at the edge just as you went into the approach of your final jump, a little voice said, "I

Mental Training Log

Event: _____ **Date:** _____

Finishing place/score: _____ **My goal:** _____

General feelings, successes, and doubts:

Positive thoughts and feelings, and what they did for me:

Negative thoughts and feelings, and how they hindered me:

How I overcame these negative thoughts:

don't think I'll ever be good enough to beat her," or maybe, "Boy, I have been right on this whole routine; she will have to work hard to beat me." When you think you have written down everything you can remember, read it over once, noticing the positive things and the negative things. Remember what you were doing when you were being positive and let go of the negative things for the time being.

Continue to keep a log for at least three or four weeks during training for a certain competition. At the end of this period, go back to the beginning of the log and read through your mental process for those weeks. Do you notice any patterns? Ask yourself the following questions:

- What were the positive thoughts and feelings I had and what did they do for me?
- What were the negative thoughts, beliefs, and feelings I had and how did they hinder me?
- Did I overcome these negative thoughts? If so, how?

Begin to analyze each performance, each entry, for similarities, differences, strengths, and weaknesses. Find out what you do in your mind that helps you perform at your peak. Become aware of the mental and emotional beliefs, reactions, and words that limit your performance. Become aware of the times you feel the most powerful and the times you feel powerless, frustrated, and out of control. Note any patterns that appear in this three- or four-week log.

It is from the entries in your log that you will form your goals and find the places you most need affirmations and visualizations to assist you in performing at your peak. The patterns you see are important in the creation of your working goals for the short, intermediate, and long term.

Identifying Your Goals

Goals are the basis of any mental training. Goal setting is the clearest way of establishing a consistent program for training and competition in your sport. It is also a powerful form of direction and motivation for both individual athletes and entire teams. The effects of a goal-setting system are cumulative. As you achieve your first goals, you will become more certain of what you want from yourself and your sport. You will also become more certain of just how to accomplish what you want. Learning to set short-term, intermediate, and long-term goals is one of the most powerful tools you can use to increase the level of your performance. Your goals become the framework that guides your training, your competitions, and your life. Your goals, whatever they may be, and your desire to achieve them are the motivation that pushes you through the rain and snow, through pain and injuries, and through the times when you feel stuck at a certain level or plateau.

A goal is anything you wish for, dream about, or choose to achieve. It can be easy, difficult, possible, or seemingly impossible. A goal is not something you make judgments about; it is simply something that you choose to pursue and achieve. Whatever your goals, they must be specific to you. They must be yours—not your parents', not your mate's, not your best friend's, and not even your coach's. Your goals must be what *you* want:

Andre Agassi, Grand Slam champion, has mastered tennis and positive thinking.

© SportsChrome

Goals must be for each individual, not for someone else. You must remember that only you have control over your own behavior. As much as you might like to change the behavior of others, you cannot. You must keep in mind that the only behavior that you can change is your own. (Harris and Harris 1984)

Setting Realistic Goals

You should set goals that you think are attainable but also challenging. You set goals to improve your level of performance, and you don't know exactly what your limits are. If you say your goal is simply to improve or to do your best, you leave too much room for confusion and lack of risk or motivation. Evaluating your present level of performance and analyzing your past will help you form goals that are realistic for you. This will also help you set goals that challenge and push you beyond what you may think is possible. Goals are sometimes the only way you can measure your progress. Therefore, it is important that your goals be measurable and specific. As you progress and begin to achieve your goals, step-by-step, you will begin to measure your success in terms of your progress rather than in terms of wins and losses. If you structure your goals in a positive way, each time you win or lose will mean that you have achieved some goal.

Think about what you wished to accomplish when you began your sport. What was it that intrigued you about it? Why did you choose your specific sport and what did you wish to accomplish? Become aware of where you are now in this sport. How has your ability changed and what do you want from yourself and your sport right now? Where are you going? Where do you want to go?

As the answers begin to come to you, write them down. Make a list of all the things you wished for in the beginning and all the things you now hope to achieve. Allow them to come randomly and write them in Mental Trainer #2. Do not give yourself time to worry about achieving these goals or about failing or succeeding. Simply put them down if they are important to you and don't analyze them further at this point. At the same time, begin to imagine what kind of difference the achievement of these goals will make in your performance or competition. What will it look like and feel like to you to accomplish these goals?

Once you have this list, begin to order and categorize your goals according to importance and time frame. Which goals are the most important to you? Which can be reached this month and which may take a year? Plan to work on two or three goals at a

Mental Trainer #2: Goaltending

Goals I wish to obtain in my sport:

30-day goals:

Definition:

6-month goals:

Definition:

1-year goals:

Definition:

time. Pick three for this month, three for the next six months, and three for the next year. To avoid feeling overwhelmed, you may want to number each goal and write an *S* for short-term, an *I* for intermediate, or an *L* for long-term next to the goal number. Short-term goals are usually those aimed at a specific workout or competition taking place within the next two weeks or even the next three days. Short-term goals tend to be very clear and specific such as, "I want to maintain an eight-minute pace throughout my entire five-mile run tomorrow," or "I want to rush the net each time I serve, being aggressive and ready throughout the entire match in the doubles competition next weekend."

Intermediate goals may be specific or they may be broad and less well defined. They are usually goals you want to reach within the next six months and may take several steps to achieve. Many times, the steps to your intermediate and long-term goals become your short-term goals.

If you try to work with more than two or three goals at one time or do not set your priorities, you may never know what you want, when you want it, or how to get it. From your list of goals, pick the three most important short-term, intermediate, and long-term goals and again use Mental Trainer #2 to keep track of your thoughts.

Now is when you should spend time analyzing exactly what you mean by each goal. What does it look like to you? Define your goals in writing as clearly as you can. This will make you aware of exactly what they mean to you and how it will feel to work for them and achieve them.

Realize that no goal is etched in stone. Your goals change as time changes, as your physical abilities change, and as your personal circumstances change. You will find that as you let go of one or two goals, new ones will quickly come to take their place. This is a natural sequence of events in your growth as an athlete.

Taking Smaller Steps

For many people, figuring out how to achieve a given goal seems overwhelming, and they sometimes resist getting started or avoid working toward any goals. If this is you, know that this feeling of frustration and confusion can be easily handled. All you have to do is take the time to think of and write down at least three steps you can take, one at a time, toward achieving each goal. These steps are actually minigoals that simplify your way to the larger goal, reducing the stress you feel when choosing to reach for a goal.

Minigoals are small steps to a larger (long-term) goal. To reach a goal, ask yourself what small steps you can take to reach it. Here are two examples of how you can break down a goal into smaller steps.

Goal: As a downhill skier, I want to take 45 seconds off my giant slalom time by the end of the season, which is five months away. This will help me move up in individual standings, make me feel more credible as an athlete, and improve my self-image.
Step 1: Prepare for and approach gates at a higher angle.
Step 2: Keep both hands in front of my shoulders at all times.
Step 3: Research and analyze all new waxes and bases for all conditions at least one week before competition.

Goal: As a middle-distance runner, I want to make nationals this year for indoor track. This means taking at least three seconds off my best time. Making the nationals would help me feel as if all the time and energy I have put into my running is finally paying off.
Step 1: Use the turns—don't be afraid of the turns and don't slow down and lose time. Attack the turns and be in control.
Step 2: Know that I am as good and as fast as anyone else on the track, and relax going into the race.
Step 3: Lengthen my stride and push harder in the backstretch instead of worrying about going out too fast and not having enough left for the finish.

Now it's your turn! Using Mental Trainer #3, list your long-term goals and define them as you did before. Then, list three minigoals or steps that will help you achieve these goals.

This exercise can be used to help you clarify and achieve all of your goals. Once you become accustomed to this process, any hesitation or lack of confidence in reaching for a goal will lessen, and you will succeed.

Understand and accept that you are not your acts, you are not your failures, and you are also not your successes. Become aware that the process of goal setting gives you a sense of direction and control over what you do and where you go in your life. This awareness requires an understanding that being successful or failing occasionally has nothing to do with your self-worth as an athlete or a human being. Few people are successful in everything

Mental Trainer #3:   Step-by-Step to Success

Goal 1: _____

Define: _____

Step 1:

Step 2:

Step 3:

Goal 2: _____

Define: _____

Step 1:

Step 2:

Step 3:

Goal 3: _____

Define: _____

Step 1:

Step 2:

Step 3:

they attempt. Being willing to risk, to reach, and to move beyond those beliefs and fears that prevent you from realizing your peak performance are your ultimate goals.

If you want something, you should "put it out there" with your intention and your energy behind it. It is important for all people, whether they are athletes or not, to have dreams and visions for the future, and who is to say what is realistic and what is not? The world of sports is full of inspirational stories of athletes who overcame unbelievable odds to succeed at the national or international level. If the odds are against you, instead of asking, "Why me?" you should ask, "Why *not* me?" Dare to dream and have a vision.

Letting Go of a Goal

How do you let go of a goal after having it for months or years? You spend hundreds of hours visualizing, affirming, and imagining yourself victorious and achieving your goals and dreams. Maybe you wanted to win the state championship or to make the Olympic team. What do you do if you don't achieve your most sacred goals? You learn to let go and surrender with style and grace. This is easy to say and sometimes hard to do. Yes, you must dream. Yes, you must follow your visions. And, if after years of hard work your ultimate dreams have eluded you, you simply have to let go, acknowledge your achievements, and go on with life, continuing to seek new pathways, new ideas, and new dreams. Remember that letting go is *not* the same as giving up. It is simply letting go, moving on, setting new goals and visions, and trusting the process of your own personal path.

The frustration of lost dreams was expressed beautifully by Liz Bradley, a member of an Olympic rowing team whom I interviewed after her Olympic experience:

> It is an emotional gamble to set goals so high: the act of doing so is what draws you along the path, but you are set up for a big disappointment if you don't attain them. We were fifth. It hurt to not get the bronze, which is where I realistically thought we should have finished. I really convinced myself, hook, line, and sinker, that we were good enough to medal. So much so that I still think it and feel extremely guilty and as if I let myself, my boat mates, team, country, parents, etc. down. I don't regret having done the mental training, because it probably got us past the Russians and into the six-boat final. Maybe we *were* good enough to expect the bronze.

Bradley was very disappointed that she didn't achieve her goals. It takes time to let go and train down from elite competition, and it takes time to set new goals and new directions in life.

Athletes may also let go of major goals when they retire from competition to pursue new careers. In these cases, the athletes apply the same discipline and training to becoming peak performers in other fields, some far from the athletic fields of their young adulthood. These athletes have learned and practiced disciplined lives for years, and their goals simply change from physical achievement to career achievement. And so it was with Bradley. She moved on, getting her PhD at MIT. When letting go of any large goal, especially at the elite level, athletes must mentally and physically train down as they let go of the unattained goal.

Training Down

Training down can be applied by any athlete who wants to let go of an unachieved goal and move, positively and constructively, toward new goals and dreams. Training down is the process of adapting to a less demanding training regimen, retiring from a sport, or taking up a new sport. The highly trained athlete must train down slowly rather than stopping strenuous exercise "cold turkey." With this process, athletes are given time physically and emotionally to let go of their goals. See table 4.1 for my own guidelines for a train-down program.

Olympic athletes often have an especially difficult time with the letdown or depression after world championship or Olympic competition. Many suffer from complete mental and physical burnout when they retire from elite competition. After years of intense training, this retirement may be a retirement from a lifestyle that has been formed for as many as 15 or 20 years. This is a huge loss—a death of a way of life.

Athletes should be encouraged to mourn this death if they need to. Many may see their retirement as a relief, but for those who see it as the death of a way of life, it needs to be treated accordingly. Some retiring athletes have described crying for no apparent reason, sleeplessness, early morning waking, and other symptoms of depression. This is compounded in retirement from sports that have a high-aerobic base. If training drops to nothing, the body reacts physically to less exercise by craving endorphins. (Endorphins are released during and after exercise and provide a feeling of extreme well-being and satisfaction. They are important in combating depressed feelings.)

Table 4.1 | Train-Down Program

Physical

- Gradually reduce workouts 10 to 15 percent weekly for a period of six weeks to two months.

- Choose a form of "maintenance" exercise to make sure your body gets some exercise and to stay in recreational shape.

- Investigate alternative exercise programs. This may be cross-training or perhaps a completely new sport to enjoy as a recreational athlete.

- Eat a healthy, low-fat, complex-carbohydrate diet with adequate protein intake. This allows you to maintain fitness, gives you plenty of energy, and keeps your weight down while doing less exercise.

- Sleep for at least eight hours a night. You may feel there is no reason to sleep so much, but your body has worked hard for years. The emotional and physical exertion has been extreme, and your body may feel the need to rest and relax.

- Get massages biweekly, or even more frequently, to induce relaxation and peacefulness in your body. This will help to nurture your body in a simple, pleasurable way.

Mental and Emotional

- Keep a journal after the Olympics or any other big competition. Write in the journal daily or every other day for one to two months. Describe your moods, feelings, ideas, and insights. This will serve to get your feelings out of your body and onto paper. The journal may turn out to be important to you in later years.

- Talk with friends and colleagues about what you are feeling; if they are fellow athletes, ask them how they are feeling and what their plans and ideas are.

- Get some personal counseling if you think it might be helpful. Talking with a professional can help you get things out. It can also assure you that your problems and concerns are reasonable rather than weird and unacceptable.

- Make a list of what you gained and learned from your experiences, including your successes and what you are happy with—all the positives.

- Make a list of regrets. Develop a process for acknowledging your feelings. Be willing to forgive yourself and let go of your regrets and shortcomings. When you complete the list, burn it, bury it, or throw it away. This small ritual can be helpful in letting go of your sorrow or your negative feelings of disappointment or anger.

- Go for career counseling and get information about what you might want to do next.

- Write affirmations about letting go of this cycle of your life; affirmations about forgiveness of yourself can be very helpful in your letting go process.

- Record and listen to the visualization in this chapter. It can help you acknowledge your feelings, let go, forgive yourself, and open up a space emotionally for something new to come into your life.

If you hide or deny your feelings, they stay with you forever. It's only by letting them go that you can be truly free. And it's only by experiencing them that you can let them go.

Retiring athletes often seem to be suffering from symptoms of post-traumatic stress disorder (PTSD). The U.S. Olympic Committee has guidelines and training programs to help athletes adapt to lifestyle changes. These train-down programs also apply to athletes who are trying to let go of a goal so that they can move on in their development as an athlete. Both groups of athletes are attempting to let go and move on in their lives. Some seek professional help to cope with their loss of lifestyle and image.

Although you haven't yet reached the point in this book that teaches you about visualizations and imagery, the visualization for letting go of a goal is presented here to give you a taste of what is to come. This will also show you the thinking processes involved in visualizations. This visualization can be applied to any situation where you are letting go of something and moving on to something new. You can make a tape of the visualizations or read them slowly, imagining and visualizing the words as you are reading.

Visualization for Letting Go

Find a comfortable place to sit or lie. Close your eyes and take a deep breath . . . holding it and letting it go. Allow yourself to begin to think about your athletic accomplishments . . . what have you done over the last five years . . . begin to see, hear, and feel your great competitive moments in their entirety . . . allow yourself to remember one of your peak performances . . . see the people who were there with you . . . hear all the sounds of that performance . . . feel the feelings in your body of that peak performance . . . the excitement, the excellence . . . the confidence and power that you felt . . . remember it all . . . and begin to acknowledge yourself, your performances . . . your abilities . . . your strengths . . . knowing that you were good, you were powerful, and you were talented in what you were doing. . . .

You deserved to be on those teams and to win and accomplish what you achieved . . . remember it all . . . knowing you were worthy of it all . . . feeling good and whole and complete . . . acknowledge your successes . . . being proud, and knowing you did the best you could . . . begin to allow yourself to let go of those memories . . . feeling your body and mind release them . . . sending them off into the air around you . . . seeing them fade slowly away into a beautiful golden light . . .

letting them go gracefully and with love and appreciation in your heart . . . gratitude for the experiences, the friends, and the places you visited and competed in . . . appreciation for the richness of your athletic life . . . allow yourself to let go of it with love. . . .

Letting go easily and without effort . . . allow yourself to forgive yourself or others for any mistakes that were made during your last performances . . . saying, "I forgive you, (saying your name) . . . it is okay to make some mistakes . . . you are forgiven . . . it is over . . . it is time to go on to new things . . . I love you, accept you, and forgive you . . . it is okay, and you are okay . . . it is okay to let go . . . ," and imagine yourself looking into a mirror, into your own eyes . . . saying, "I forgive you . . . ," and knowing that it is time to forgive and let go . . . let all the images fade into a golden light . . . and feel your mind and your heart being open and receptive . . . allowing yourself to make room for something new in your life . . . allowing yourself to be open . . . open-minded . . . openhearted . . . allowing the space in your mind and heart to be open to new possibilities and new dreams . . . enjoy this new and open feeling . . . knowing that it is okay to wait for something new to come in . . . perhaps now, perhaps later as you are doing some other activity, something new will come in. . . .

Know you are now just preparing yourself for new adventures . . . a new you and a new life . . . knowing that all the learning you received by being a competitive athlete prepared you for many other aspects of your life . . . acknowledging again what a gift it was to have had your opportunities . . . begin looking forward to the future with trust and anticipation . . . knowing and trusting that you will receive . . . and that you will be blessed by some new and unexpected adventure . . . trusting the continuing process of abundance and prosperity in your life . . . being open and receptive to the process of change. . . .

Imagining the golden light surrounding you, protecting you . . . knowing you are safe . . . trusting yourself and trusting the process of change . . . begin to become aware of your body sitting in the chair, or lying down . . . and on a count of three, you may open your eyes, feeling alert, awake, and ready for the rest of the day or evening . . . knowing it is okay to let go of the past and to look toward your future . . . with anticipation and excitement . . . knowing that you have within you

> everything you need to be, do, and have what you want in life . . . knowing you are flexible, able to receive and let go gracefully. . . .
>
> One . . . move your hands and feet . . . taking a deep breath . . . letting it out . . . two . . . move your neck and head, stretching your shoulders and neck . . . and three . . . open your eyes when you're ready . . . feeling alert and awake.

Whether you're setting a goal or letting go of a goal, staying positive is a very important skill to learn. Learning to write and use affirmations or positive self-statements is important in constructing a mind-set of positive thinking.

Talking Positively

Positive thinking is important to goal setting and letting go. The negative thoughts you have are a product of outside influences that continually tell you that you're not good enough. Over a period of time, you begin to believe that you're not good enough.

Your life is spent thinking, even if you are not aware of it. Your mind has about 10 million thoughts per day. At least as many of these thoughts are negative as are positive.

When you were born, your spirit was free of belief systems. You had no concept of fear, love, rejection, competence, acceptance, hate, and so on. You were taught. You were taught to be gentle, to love, to risk, to know what can hurt you, and to limit yourself. For the most part, you were unconscious of this learning process. Over the years your parents, teachers, peers, neighbors, churches, bosses, and friends have told you such things as, "Be careful crossing the street or you'll get hurt," "You can't do that," "Girls don't do that sort of thing," "Being an athlete makes you a man," "Your body is bad and dirty," "Love is better than war," "Feelings make you weak," "Don't cry," "At the end of every rainbow is a pot of gold," "Be afraid of strangers," "Winning is everything," and on and on. Sound familiar?

First, you should know that whatever your belief system, it was learned and can be unlearned. Second, you should become aware of what beliefs work for you, supporting your spirit and usefulness in the world, and what beliefs limit you, defeat you, and cause you pain. It makes a lot of sense to be careful when crossing the street or to be wary of strangers. But as a woman, does it work for you to believe that women are too weak to participate in some sports or that it is unfeminine to be better than the boys? As a man, does it work for you to believe that if you are not interested in sports, or not very good at them, that you are less of a man? Does it work for you to believe that you can't do something? Does it work for you to believe that if you don't win you are a failure?

So, how did successful athletes get to the point where they let go of their negative thoughts? Some athletes were always positive and upbeat; they intuitively knew they were good, competent, and strong and that it was perfectly acceptable for them to reach for any goal they chose. And some athletes taught themselves to be positive because they found it worked, little by little, to believe in themselves. The latter may be the major reason you are reading this book. How you hold yourself in your heart and mind is how you perform in life in general. What you believe to be true about yourself determines your successes, your failures, your ability to

Let positive thinking be your guide.

risk, your strength to handle any situation, and ultimately, how you treat yourself and others.

Think of your last two or three competitions or workouts. Were they good? Or did you fall short of your goal? As you were performing, and for the 24 hours afterward, what was going on in your head? What, if anything, were you saying to yourself? Think of what you say to yourself on a day-to-day basis. Does it sound something like this: "Oh, you stupid idiot . . . how could you do such a dumb thing?" or "You'll never beat that person . . . just look at how strong he is," or "No way can I perform well in this weather or when all these people are watching me."

A young woman in one of my workshops described how her performance was affected by what she told herself:

> Every time I show up at the track for a competition, I am so tired, I have no energy, no motivation. It's like I just don't want to be there, like I'm bored or something. I'd say things to myself such as, "Oh come on . . . you can't win if you're always so lazy!" and "What makes you think you can even run when you are bored and acting so stupid?" When I start to get on my case about feeling that way, everything tightens up and I usually don't do very well.

Keep in mind that your thoughts control and sometimes dictate your emotions. Take a minute to think about your self-talk and self-concept, and then begin Mental Trainer #4.

Now, as you begin to have a clearer picture of what you say to yourself, read the positive things again and relate them to your performance. Notice how they helped you to stay focused, to push ahead, to try harder, or simply to feel good about your performance and therefore yourself. Now read the negative thoughts. Notice if there were more negative thoughts than positive, when they occurred, and what happened to your focus, your form, and your performance when you listened to them and kept them in your conscious mind. How did they distract, limit, or defeat you?

Affirmations

Positive self-statements (affirmations) are powerful weapons you can use to combat the destructive self-beliefs and self-talk you confront during workouts and, more important, during competitions. For most people, there are fleeting periods of nervousness or self-doubt. Those are the times to use an affirmation to change your focus and energy. Affirmations will short-circuit the negative talk.

Mental Trainer #4:   My Self-Talk

What I say to myself before a workout:

Positive

Negative

What I say to myself before a competition:

Positive

Negative

What I say to myself after a competition:

Positive

Negative

An affirmation is a positive self-statement that usually is not true at the time but supports what you want to be true. An affirmation supports the way you want to view yourself and your abilities, or it supports a goal you want to achieve during the specific workout or competition.

Affirmations are always positive, present tense, and personal. Affirmations are positive because the subconscious does not take in negatives, and they are positive because that is the whole idea—to change the doubt or destructive thought into one that supports and enriches your confidence, self-concept, and performance. Affirmations are present tense because it is very important to be in the here and now. They are something you want to believe is true right now. And an affirmation is always personal. You have control only over yourself, no one else. By using positive self-statements, you are working on changing your personal belief systems, your destructive self-concepts. Table 4.2 includes examples of affirmations for letting go of goals.

Table 4.2 Affirmations for Letting Go of a Goal

- I let go of my goals for _____ and open myself to new possibilities.

- I acknowledge my strength and learning gained in the process of going for my goals.

- I did the best I could do in striving for my goal.

- It is easy for me to let go of the past and look toward the future.

- I am enjoying the present.

- I am taking care of myself, resting, and relaxing.

- It is time for me to move on to new challenges.

- I find new things to inspire and challenge me in new ways.

- It is okay for me to feel sad or depressed. I am mourning the passing of a way of life for me.

- I am proud of my dedication and achievements in my competitive years.

- I acknowledge myself and my abilities.

- Being ranked ____ in the world is a fine achievement.

- I am proud of myself and the goals that I achieved.

- We all did the best we could do during the competition.

- My future is filled with abundance and prosperity.

- I trust and believe in myself.

- I let go of the past and move on.

- I forgive myself with love and acceptance.

- My mind and body are at peace.

- I am grateful for my healthy body, my good mind, and my fitness.

- I am grateful for all the support I received from my family, teammates, friends, and coaches.

- I am grateful for my achievements and honors, my energy and creativity, and the opportunity to compete at world-class levels.

- I am grateful for the abundance in my life.

What you want to do is change negative thoughts so they support you and help you to know that you are in control. Affirmations are "I am" statements. They are the reverse of your negative, limiting self-talk. You may not feel that they are true at this moment. When you were learning all the limiting self-beliefs, they were also untrue, but because you bought the idea—someone else's idea—you made these beliefs part of your own reality. You now know that you can create your own reality. You can create a positive, unlimited, supportive self-reality. It's a matter of buying a new set of beliefs, beliefs that are positive and self-nurturing.

Take a look at your negative thoughts from Mental Trainer #4. How can you make these positive, present tense, and personal? Now, use Mental Trainer #5 to help turn your previously negative thoughts into positive self-statements.

The harder it is to form a positive statement from one of your negative beliefs, the better it will be for you, and the more important it is to change it to a positive self-statement. For example, you may write, "I am strong and confident and capable of beating anyone at this competition." When you write this, if it feels strange in the pit of your stomach, or if you laugh and shake your head, or if it is difficult to write down and say to yourself, then it

Mental Trainer #5:   Transformers

Negative thought 1:

Positive affirmation: I am _____

_____.

Negative thought 2:

Positive affirmation: I am _____

_____.

Negative thought 3:

Positive affirmation: I am _____

_____.

is perfect for you. It is an important one for you. Here are some more examples:

> I believe in my own ability as an athlete.
>
> I have a positive mental attitude and self-image.
>
> I believe in myself.
>
> The more I believe in myself, the better I perform.
>
> I am strong and powerful.
>
> I am in control and focused.
>
> I love to compete and push myself, reaching for my goals.
>
> I am prepared and relaxed.
>
> I enjoy performing before a crowd and appreciate their support.
>
> I am a capable and competent athlete.
>
> I *am* good enough.
>
> It is okay to make mistakes. I learn from them and I am stronger.

Once you have changed all your negative thoughts into affirmations, write your old, negative statements on a piece of paper. Now physically get rid of them. You may want to burn the paper or bury it. Maybe you could put it in a bottle and send it out to sea or perhaps give it to your dog to eat. Whatever you do, release yourself from these thoughts and bring your focus back to the positive statements and beliefs that are now becoming part of your reality.

Now go back to Mental Trainer #2 and find your original goals. Read them again and think of how you are going to achieve each of them and what you wish to experience at that point. Pick one from each group—one short-term, one intermediate, and one long-term—and use Mental Trainer #6 to help you develop at least three affirmations that support each of these goals. For example, if your short-term goal was to stay on the balance beam throughout your entire routine, to feel in control and light, and to make it all the way through, your affirmations may look like this:

1. I am balanced and in control.
2. I am performing perfectly throughout my entire routine.
3. I am light and controlled, staying on the beam through my whole routine.

Mental Trainer #6:   Goaling Forward

Short-term goal:

Affirmations:

Intermediate goal:

Affirmations:

Long-term goal:

Affirmations:

You should go through this process each time you make a goal for yourself. Positive self-statements support what you wish to achieve and help you change your negative belief systems to positive. As a result, they cause you to put out a positive intent to the world around you. Your control of and gradual belief in this positive intent is what begins to change your reality. The more you support yourself and your athletic endeavors, the more the world around you will support you. Achieving your goals will become easier and easier.

Read over the affirmations you just wrote. Are you using *can* or *will* in your sentences? Have you written, "I will always be in control and focused?" or "I can stay on the beam without falling?" The use of words such as *can* and *will* puts your intent too far in the future. It causes your mind to believe that it will always have time and gives it an excuse for not believing in your reality; your reality is always out there somewhere and you remain only partially in control. It is always better to use sentences that are in the present tense such as, "I am in control and focused," or "I stay on the beam with excellent balance." In the present tense, the mind accepts these thoughts as already true, not as conditional statements or wishes for the future. In the present tense, the words are already true and they go into your brain as such.

You may review your list of goals only once a week or so, but it is important to read your affirmations at least twice a day. The best times to read them are at night before you turn out your light and in the morning before you start your day. These are times when you are relaxed and your mind is uncluttered. When you are the most relaxed, your subconscious is the most open to receiving new ideas and beliefs. And, the deeper you are able to receive these positive self-statements, the sooner they become reality.

Once you are familiar with your affirmations, you will find there are many times in your daily life when they come in handy. If you feel tired or sore in a competition, or if self-doubt begins to creep into your thoughts as you perform, reach inside for these positive statements, and they will help you maintain focus, confidence, and control. They will help you believe you can push yourself further, reach higher, run longer or faster, and move beyond any self-imposed limitations. Though it is important to acknowledge pain or fatigue, it is ultimately important to go beyond it, to release it, and to focus on the positive to reach your peak performance.

Saying nice things to yourself is not bragging or showing false pride. It is building a solid sense of self-worth and self-acceptance. It is part of being on your own team. Acknowledgment of yourself and your abilities is important in supporting your self-confidence. Muhammad Ali said, "In order to be a great champion, you must believe that you are the best . . . and if you're not, pretend that you are." Though Ali was not always the most humble of athletes, he believed in himself. He had one of the best affirmations of all time, "I am the greatest!" And he was.

Ultimately, it never matters what others are thinking. You can do nothing about that. But you can change your own belief systems, put yourself at ease, and restore your own self-confidence. This chapter has led you through the mental log process and helped you write goals and affirmations in the present tense as if they were already true. As you repeat your goals as affirmations, your subconscious and unconscious minds absorb and retain these thoughts, and your thinking is reprogrammed into becoming more positive and supportive.

Chapter 5

Preparing Your Mind and Body for Mental Training

Relaxation is the supreme nourishment for the body, mind, and soul.

For many people, the hardest task in athletics and in life is to know who or what helps them feel good about themselves and their world, that is, who or what promotes a state of relaxation and well-being. The second most difficult task is achieving a state of balance—balance between training and rest, between work and play, between seriousness and spontaneity, and between relaxation and readiness. People get caught up in what they have to do, or should do, or should be. This imbalance costs them a lot.

You know that the more relaxed and at ease you are, the more you feel in balance and the better your performance, whether in sport, at work or school, in your relationships, or in your creative endeavors. But how do you achieve this balance? How do you find and maintain this kind of harmony within yourself so that you can achieve your peak performance? One step is to become aware of the activities, the people, and the places that give you joy, peace, support, learning, and growth. People seem to be very good at knowing all the things, situations, people, and so on that make them feel insecure, angry, or frustrated with themselves. But people seldom take the time to be honest and self-nurturing enough to really connect with all the things that add to their lives and that balance the more negative things to which they seem so attached. To be an effective and successful athlete, you should know who and what promote your centeredness, confidence, relaxation, and your ability to have fun. Mental Trainer #7 will help you become more aware of these people and things.

Mental Trainer #7: What Makes Me Feel Good

1. List all the things you like to do. List the things that give you happiness and confidence. Include the things you may not allow yourself to do because they make you feel so good that something inside tells you it's not okay to be so happy.

2. List all the people you enjoy being with, sharing with, and giving to. These are the people who put you at ease. Though you may see each other infrequently, still it feels natural and easy each time you get together. They are people who support and care about you in their hearts and toward whom you feel the same.

3. With these lists in mind, complete the following drawing. Include both the people and the activities or things from the above lists. Fill in the circles closest to you with those people or things you consider to be the closest, most important, or most nourishing to you. Those you feel least strongly about will go in the circles farthest from you. Think clearly and deeply about each one. What does this person really mean to you, and what does he or she give or receive from you and your relationship that helps build the peace and happiness within yourself? Ask the same questions of the activities or things you enjoy.

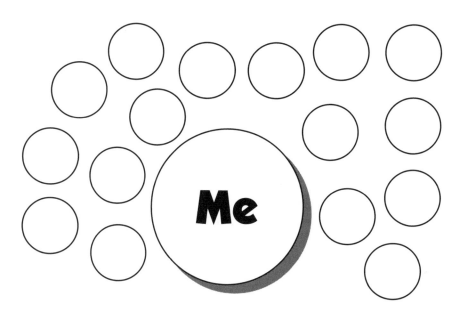

4. Are you surprised by some of the things or people you included? Are you amazed at how good it feels to connect with that thing or person that brings joy and relaxation to your life?

5. The next step is to give yourself permission to, at least once a week, enjoy being with one of these nourishing people or do one of those things that delights you. This means making and taking the time to give yourself a relaxing, stress-reducing, self-supporting gift once a week regardless of how busy you are. This will keep you fresh and motivated mentally.

Simply learn to relax, take care of yourself, and find balance in your life and sport. Performing at your peak is next to impossible when you are stressed, tired, and "out of sorts." Living a life free of serious illness or injury is also difficult if you are unwilling to slow down, rest, quiet your mind, and find the peace in each day. In the world of mental training, another important reason to learn to relax is that it helps you prepare for a visualization—the process of creating images in your mind. When you are about to perform a visualization, which you will learn more about in chapter 6, it is important to induce your body into a state of quiet relaxation. This creates a receptivity in the mind that enhances the depth of the visualization. If you are relaxed, the visualization can be taken in more deeply, and it will become more a part of you. Because visualizations are so powerful, the more relaxed you are, the more

I am relaxed, focused, and alert.

© Empics

your subconscious believes it has experienced the created images in reality. What the mind imagines, the body produces.

Learning to relax and nurture yourself is healthy and energy inducing whether you do it for stress reduction, healing, balance, visualization preparation, or simply to slow down and enjoy life to a fuller plane. The more positive things you do for yourself—for example, the more you allow yourself to enjoy the company of those who support you for the person you are—the fewer negative things you will do against yourself. The more positive changes that occur, the better you will feel about yourself. You will become more and more aware of and confident in your ability to control the forces affecting your performance and your life.

Finding Balance Through Relaxation

Using certain exercises to relax and find balance is one of the more positive things you can do for your body and your mind. If, for some reason, you have come up with only one or two things you enjoy doing to help you relax and feel good, this chapter provides several suggestions. I have found these methods to be most beneficial to the athletes I have worked with. To begin to understand what it takes for you to relax, not only in life, but also during major workouts and competitions, give yourself permission to try some of these methods.

Breathing Deeply

Breathe! Sounds easy, right? Everyone breathes. Not everyone, however, uses breathing to his or her advantage, especially in athletics. More important, not everyone uses breathing to relax and renew energy before, during, and after competition. Correct breathing is one of the most valuable techniques an athlete can learn for focusing, calming, and energizing.

Diaphragmatic, or belly, breathing is the easiest form of breathing to learn. As you free your breath through diaphragmatic breathing, you relax your emotions and let go of your body tensions. Your belly rises and falls as your lungs are fully inflated, and your diaphragm stays loose and flexible. Breathing is rhythmic and deep. Because most people are thoracic (chest) breathers, it may take some practice for you to learn to fill your belly area completely with each breath, easily inhaling and exhaling without forcing your abdominal muscles to expand and contract.

Diaphragmatic breathing increases the amount of oxygen taken into your bloodstream and therefore increases the amount available to your muscles. A greater amount of air is exchanged when you breathe deeply, causing your breathing rhythm to slow and become steadier. This, in turn, calms your nerves and steadies your emotions, bringing about relaxation and a sense of control.

Proper diaphragmatic breathing involves the entire torso. It is useful to envision this breathing pattern as a three-step process. First, the diaphragm moves downward, creating a vacuum in the chest cavity that draws air into the lower portions of the lungs. Next, the middle part of the lungs begins to inflate, and the abdominal area expands . . . from just below the rib cage to just above the navel. Finally, the chest itself expands, filling the upper portion of the lungs (Garfield 1984).

When exhaling, follow these same steps: empty your abdominal area first, then the middle part of the lungs, and finally the chest and upper lungs. Each time you exhale, imagine letting go of old and stale energy, air, tiredness, and tightness. Become empty and ready to receive new and clean air, energy, and relaxation. Inhale, feeling new, vital strength flowing in . . . exhale, releasing old tiredness and tenseness. You can also silently say to yourself, "Inhale new energy, exhale old energy," or "Strength in, tiredness out," or "Power and strength in, tension out."

When people are afraid, nervous, or worried, they tend to restrict their breathing, holding it tightly high in their chest or even in their throats. This cuts off normal oxygenation and causes them to feel fatigue and to lose physical coordination and mental concentration. Becoming aware of your breathing, and focusing on its rhythm and depth, will enhance your energy, your control, your concentration, and ultimately your performance.

Meditating Quietly

Meditation is a clearing and quieting of the mind. Thoughts are focused in one quiet direction, and all other distractions, chatter, and ideas are released. Meditation initiates a general decrease in your metabolism, heart rate, and breathing rate. It also causes an overall decline in your body's need to utilize oxygen. Therefore, reserve using meditation for times when you do not expect to be immediately physically active. Meditation is an excellent way to relax the night before competition if you find sleep or a sense of peace difficult to achieve. Meditation helps diminish muscular tension in the major muscle groups and helps you to restore body balance before and after intense physical activity.

Find a quiet time and place, a place where you are comfortable both physically and mentally, and sit or lie in a relaxed posture that supports your body. Close your eyes and think of a few words or sounds that take little effort to say, such as "relaxed," "peaceful," "calm," or "quiet." Breathing deeply and quietly, begin saying these words in rhythm over and over, gearing them to the ebb and flow of your breathing. Focus only on the words until your mind becomes empty of all else. Be aware momentarily of the physical relaxation as it slowly moves over you and you begin to disconnect from your body, staying focused only on the sounds and their rhythm. Continue your meditation for 10 or 15 minutes, allowing nothing to distract you or enter your mind except the words you are repeating. Let it be. Some of the greatest performances in sports come when the mind is still as a deep lake, and the athlete is in a zone of effortless performance.

When you feel fully at peace and very physically relaxed, begin to reconnect with your body. Slowly and gently move your head to the right and then to the left and to the center. Breathing quietly, open your eyes and your mind to the space you are occupying.

If you meditate before bed to relax and prepare for sleep, you may find that you fall asleep easily. This is the purpose of your meditation. If your mind wanders, continue to work at keeping your focus on specific sounds or words. Don't worry. With practice, you will learn to stay focused. You will learn to use this form of relaxation anywhere and anytime you need to quiet and clear your mind in order to focus your attention where you want it.

You may also want to experiment with tai chi chuan, a form of physical or moving meditation. In this practice, the body is taught and allowed to find a quiet, rhythmic movement containing strength, balance, concentration of mind and body, and patience. Each movement should be synchronized with the rhythm of total movement.

For example, stand with your right foot slightly ahead of and apart from your left foot, finding a comfortable balance and control. Find a spot or focal point straight ahead and hold your visual attention there. With all your body parts aligned over your center (two inches below your navel), your knees slightly bent, and your eyes fixed on one point ahead of you, move forward onto your right foot, leaving your left foot entirely on the floor. Then rock back your weight onto your left foot, leaving your right foot completely on the floor. Exhale as you move forward, and inhale as you move back to your left foot. With your elbows at your sides and your forearms parallel to the ground, palms down, slowly "push" away from your body as you move forward to your right foot. Rotate your palms until they are facing up, and slowly, as if scooping, "pull" them toward you as you rock back on your left foot bringing new energy to your body. Rotate your hands again, palms away from your body, and push as you exhale and move forward onto your right foot; rotate, palms up, and pull toward yourself as you inhale and rock to your left foot. Repeat this movement over and over, establishing a rhythm and emptying your mind and body of all other thoughts or physical distractions. Become one with the movement and rhythm of your breathing. Focus on your center and feel the energy radiating to all parts of your body.

Relieving Tension

Few things give more relief from tension and minor physical soreness or tightness than a good, deep massage. No matter where you live, there is probably at least one licensed masseur or masseuse nearby who is qualified to rub, knead, and otherwise manipulate your muscles to stimulate circulation and create relaxation of tenseness and soreness.

If you, as an athlete, are seriously active every day, you will benefit from having a massage at least once a week. You will find your body has more energy, is ready and balanced, and performs at a higher level if you stop carrying around areas of tightness and stress in your muscles. A consistent massage program will also help you remain injury free by loosening, warming, and relaxing all muscles and reducing your tension level.

Performing Yoga

There are many types of yoga available in classes and on videos. Yoga teaches focus, concentration, deep stretching, and relaxation of the mind and body. It is an excellent practice for athletes because it helps them stretch consistently in a program that is easy to follow. With yoga, an athlete can achieve excellent results with respect to flexibility, strength, and relaxation. Some of the more popular types of yoga are hatha, kundalini, vinyasa, and ashtanga. Each type has a different quality of exertion and different exercises. Yoga emphasizes breathing, mind and body relaxation, and letting go of extraneous thoughts, resulting in peace and harmony. You should sample the different types of yoga until you find the one that you and your body like best.

Floating Away

Though sensory deprivation tanks have been used since the 1930s, only recently have they been widely available to the general public. Today, they are called floatation tanks. Present-day tanks look something like a plastic egg. A floatation tank is approximately 6 feet by 9 feet, and is filled with about 12 inches of water and more than 100 pounds of Epsom salts, making it impossible for the body to sink.

Once you are in the tank, relax! Rest your body and your mind for a few minutes. You can close your eyes or leave them open. Open your thoughts to anything that comes. Let go and relax as you float effortlessly and weightlessly. There are no sounds, no feelings, no smells—only darkness. Let yourself become a container, empty and unused. Slowly become aware of any stimuli such as sports images or colors before your eyes, or a sense of turning or lightness. Notice these things, enjoy them, let them go, and remain empty and at peace.

If you are training for a specific competition, floating is the perfect time to say your affirmations or begin visualizations and mental rehearsals. Because you are so totally relaxed, your affirmations and visualizations will move further than usual into your subconscious. Your mind is more receptive and your subconscious more vulnerable to what you want it to learn.

When you leave the tank and go on with your day, you will notice a renewed energy along with a feeling of total relaxation. A float twice a month is recommended to maintain balance and to center yourself. This will help you be more deeply relaxed and create a deeper level of visualization.

Relaxing Progressively

Progressive relaxation is another form of physical relaxation that, in turn, relaxes the mind. This form focuses on the major muscle groups of the body by tensing and relaxing each of these groups one at a time. Progressive relaxation is the most common form of relaxation used before visualizing because it effectively produces deep relaxation of both the mind and the body. Another reason for using this method before visualizing is that it establishes awareness and a deep, calm breathing pattern. Progressive relaxation can be done anywhere and anytime you have a few minutes of quiet.

There are two forms of progressive relaxation: the long, total body process, and the shorter, more immediate form that can be used after you are thoroughly familiar with the long form. One of these two forms of relaxation should be done before the visualizations in this book. You can use the short form if it is easy for you to relax. If you find it hard to relax, use the long form.

Long Form

Find a quiet, comfortable place to sit or lie. You will need about 10 to 15 minutes. Sit comfortably in the chair with both your feet flat on the floor. Relax, with your hands at ease in your lap and your back against the back of the chair. If you are lying on the floor, rest with your arms at your sides, your legs fully extended, and your back flat. Begin to relax, center your body parts, and clear your mind. Centering means aligning all your body parts so that they are well supported and balanced with each other. Imagining your center of gravity and power located two inches below your navel will make you feel calm and relaxed and will enhance your sense of balance and strength. Progressive relaxation is started on your dominant side. If you are right handed, start with your right arm. If you are left handed, begin by tensing your left arm. Close your eyes and focus on your breathing. Inhale deeply into your diaphragm . . . hold it for a moment . . . and exhale from your belly up to your chest. Inhale . . . hold . . . exhale. Empty your mind, allowing any random thoughts to pass through. Feel your body and mind letting go. Inhale . . . hold it . . . exhale.

Beginning with your dominant hand, forearm, and bicep, make a fist (not too tight), hold it, feeling the tension in your arm, and let it go, completely relaxing. Make a fist of your other hand . . . hold it . . . let go. Moving to your head, tense your forehead, your nose, and your jaw, squeezing your eyebrows together . . . hold . . . and let the tension go, feeling it float away from your consciousness. Breathe. Hunch your shoulders up around your ears . . . hold . . . let them go and feel a sense of relaxation begin to flow downward, over your belly, past your hips, down your legs, and into the floor. Allow yourself to let go on a deeper and deeper level with each re-laxation. Slowly begin to roll your head to the right . . . to the front . . . and to the left. Pause. Move your head slowly to the front . . . and to the right . . . back to the front . . . and relax with your head comfortably resting on your neck. Breathe and move your awareness to your abdominal area. Slowly contract your abdominal muscles, pulling them back toward your spine . . . hold . . . and release with a sigh. Now focus on your dominant leg. Push your heel into the floor . . . hold, feeling the tightness in your thigh . . . let go. Point your toes ahead of you, feeling your calf tightening . . . hold . . . release. Move slowly to your other leg. Push your heel into the floor . . . hold . . . release. Point your toes ahead of you . . . hold . . . release, feeling all tension and connection with your body leaving your awareness. Breathe deeply . . . exhale. Inhale new energy and vitality; exhale tiredness and tension.

Short Form

This shorter form of progressive relaxation can be done any-where. It can also be used before a visualization once you have mastered the ability to totally relax yourself physically. This form may take as little as two to three minutes or as long as seven minutes depending on your desires and the time available to you. Take a quiet moment, close your eyes, and center on your breathing. Breathe in deeply and hold it for a moment, letting go and allowing your mind and body to relax and become empty and peaceful. Inhale . . . hold . . . exhale.

Move your awareness inside and notice if there are any ar-eas of tightness or places where you feel sore or uncomfortable. Begin on your dominant side and check in with each muscle group. If you feel some tension or soreness, acknowledge it, send it some energy and peace, and let it go. Move your aware-ness from side to side and from head to foot, acknowledging any tension or tightness and any pain or discomfort, sending care and energy and letting go. Return to your breathing any time you find it difficult to let go or move beyond some pain or tension. Re-center yourself and then go back to that area and let it go, allowing it to relax and become soft.

When you feel fully relaxed and centered, you are ready to begin a visualization, or you may begin to reconnect with reality by moving your fingers and toes and slowly opening your eyes. This short technique for relaxing is ideal for just before and after competition. It is also recommended for any stress-inducing situation such as before an exam, when you feel overwhelmed at work, or when a relationship is stressful and there is a need for calm, controlled communication.

Achieving Your Peak

Because life tends to place more stress on you than you feel capable of coping with from time to time, any form of relaxation is vital to your mental and physical health and well-being. Whether you choose to simply go to a movie with your best friend, take a walk, spend twenty minutes doing tai chi or yoga, or float in a tank, nourishing yourself both in mind and body will bring balance and focus to your athletic performance. Relaxation techniques can bring a high level of control to your life and help you reach any peak performance you choose. Relaxation is one of the five tools for mental training because it causes the mind and body to be more open to the peak performance visualizations. It also helps you to let go of the constant pressure to achieve that many athletes feel every day. Relaxation reduces the mental and physical intensity of hard training and lets you "chill" and have fun.

Chapter 6

Unleashing the Power of the Mind

What you see is what you get.

Flip Wilson

Some people can "see" within their mind. This means they can actually see a picture. Some see this picture from within, seeing their performance as if they are in their own body and looking out. They see the track in front of them as they run or the balance beam before them as they mount to begin their routine. Others see from without; in other words, they watch themselves perform. To be able to do both would be optimum; however, few people know how. But if you are willing to work at it, and you give yourself time, you can learn to see both ways.

Some athletes have strong physical "feelings." They are more aware of how a performance feels than what the performance looks like. When they visualize, they don't see a picture; instead, they have a feeling, a gut reaction, a physical response or memory. Others may visualize and experience their performance by how it sounds—the crowd, the voices within, the words of support from teammates, the footsteps of the runner behind them, the music and rhythm they perform to or hear during a game, and so on. For them there may be no real picture, but rather sounds, music, or a rhythm in their mind that guides them in their performance.

This visualization or imagery process is the most important of the five tools used in mental training. Your mind is one of your greatest gifts. You have the power to create your own reality with the thoughts and images in your mind. The images, feelings, and sounds you have in your mind's eye hold incredible power. They help you to risk making changes, to understand how to deal with difficulty, and to create and clarify your thoughts. How you view yourself—your abilities, your acceptability, your intelligence, your worth—ultimately determines who you become, what you do, and what you have; in other words, your reality. Having a vision for the future greatly increases the possibility of realizing your hopes and dreams.

Beginning to Visualize

How do you learn? Do you see images, or hear sounds, or feel the feelings and sensations of a peak performance? The first step in visualizing or imaging is to determine how you learn and store information. The following questionnaire will help you discover which of your senses you use most effectively for learning. Mark the appropriate option to complete each sentence with the one that describes you best.

How Do You Learn?

1. My emotions can often by interpreted from my
   a. facial expressions
   b. voice quality
   c. general body tone

2. I keep up with current athletic events by
   a. reading the sports page thoroughly when I have time
   b. listening to the news, ESPN, or TV
   c. quickly reading the sports page, spending a few minutes watching TV, or going on the Internet

3. If I wish to communicate with another person, I prefer
   a. meeting face-to-face or writing letters
   b. the telephone, cell phone, or e-mail because it saves time
   c. to get together while working out or doing something physical

4. When I am angry, I usually
   a. clam up and give others the silent treatment
   b. am quick to let others know
   c. clench my fists or grasp something tightly and storm off

5. When working out or competing, I
   a. frequently look around to see the environment or my competition
   b. tune in to what's going on in my mind or think of a song
   c. continually move around and physically get into it immediately

6. I consider myself
   a. a precise and orderly person
   b. a sensible person
   c. a physical person

7. When attending an athletic event, I
   a. come prepared to keep times and scores
   b. bring a small radio to hear the event better
   c. move around a lot and don't stay in my seat

8. In my spare time, I would rather
   a. watch TV, go to a movie, read, or surf the net
   b. listen to the radio or CDs or play an instrument
   c. participate in some physical activity

9. The best approach to disciplining an athlete is
   a. to isolate the athlete by separating him or her from the group
   b. to reason with the athlete and discuss the situation
   c. to use acceptable punishment such as benching or not competing in a game

10. The most effective way to reward an athlete is
    a. written compliments or posting recognition for others to see
    b. oral praise to the athlete in front of others
    c. a pat on the back or a hug to show appreciation

Now count the number of checks for each letter (a, b, and c). If you selected (a) most often, you are primarily a visual learner. Having the most checks for option (b) means you are mostly auditory and that you learn more through listening to sounds and rhythm. More checks for the (c) option indicates that you are a kinesthetic learner—a person who feels things and likes a hands-on learning experience. If you have about the same number of checks for two or all three of the letters, you tend to use two (or all three) methods during any learning process.

For purposes of this book, the term *visualizing* can mean all three: visual, auditory, and kinesthetic imagery. These are sensory ways in which people learn and experience what they do and what happens to them. Going into a workout or competition, if you visualize yourself as a mediocre athlete, or see yourself performing on an average level, or slower or less perfectly than those around you, or you feel you are not good enough, this is the way you will perform in reality. If, on the other hand, you visualize yourself performing well, feel that you are well prepared and ready, and hear inner talk that supports you and your ability, you will produce the experience you are aiming for.

In an athletic event, visualizing yourself performing perfectly and achieving exactly what you want becomes that added edge you need to reach your peak performance. Each time you see yourself performing exactly the way you want to perform, you physically create neural patterns in your brain. These patterns are like small tracks permanently engraved on your brain cells, and it is your brain that gives the signal to your muscles to move. Your brain tells each muscle when to move, and how much power to move with.

Numerous studies have confirmed the fact that vividly experienced imagery, imagery that is both seen and felt, can substantially affect brain waves, blood flow, heart rate, skin temperature, gastric secretions, and immune response . . . in fact, the total physiology (Houston 1997).

Athletes who have never performed a certain feat before have demonstrated that they can, after several specific visualization experiences over a period of weeks or months, perform that feat very skillfully. Ed Boyd, the former women's gymnastics coach at the University of Oregon, told of an experience where he taught a young gymnast a very difficult routine entirely by visualization. When she executed it perfectly the first time she tried, it frightened him so badly he didn't try visualization for years afterward!

When you visualize, you compete only in your mind, but this can have such a powerful effect that your entire body feels as if you have actually competed physically. Physical performance improves because your mind can't distinguish between a visualized and an actual experience. To your brain, a neural pattern is a neural pattern whether it is created by a physical act or a mental act. Your brain sends the message to the muscles, and the muscles react.

You must do the physical training—moving your body, strengthening your body, and training your body. But your performance will be tremendously more powerful if you also train your mind and create the neural patterns to help your muscles do exactly what you want them to do.

Creating a Visualization

A visualization starts at the beginning of your routine or workout. You must know what you want and what results you are aiming for in a visualization. You should know the terms and idioms that are part of the language of your sport, and you should have a clear picture of how it looks, feels, or sounds to perform perfectly in your event. You can get this picture by watching the best athletes in your sport (in person or on television) or by looking at sports pictures (in magazines or on posters). Hang pictures of athletes performing your event to perfection where you can see them as often as possible. Watch videos of top athletes in your sport performing at their best. Make a video of your own flawless performances. All of this will continually work to create the perfect picture in your mind, the perfect feeling in your body, and the perfect sounds or words in your ears. It will also keep you connected with what it will take for you to be the best you can be.

Once you have established one of your goals and written supporting affirmations, you are ready to begin creating the content of a specific visualization. When you are first learning to create visualizations, you should write them down as you go along. This will help you incorporate as many senses as possible and enable you to read them several times before you start using them. Also, you may find it helpful to have someone read the visualization to you while you are in a relaxed state, or you may want to record it yourself and listen to it later in a quiet and peaceful space.

In as much detail as possible, see in your mind's eye the whole process and routine of your event in competition or in a significant workout. Visualize the competition area, feel the weather or the atmosphere of the room, the temperature, the sounds, the smells . . . everything. Imagine yourself warming up, stretching, talking to friends, concentrating—everything you do as part of your

I am a powerful athlete.

© SportsChrome

routine just prior to competing or working out. Feel yourself being totally relaxed, confident, and in complete control of your body and your mental state. If you notice that you are nervous, remember your affirmations, and say them to yourself. For example, "I am strong and ready," or "I am relaxed and prepared."

Imagine yourself beginning to compete, beginning your routine, the race, the match, or the game. Notice everything you do, seeing it perfectly just the way you want it to be, just the way it should be done. If you make a mistake while visualizing your performance, go back, rewind, slow down the image in your mind, and do it over again, correctly, perfectly, exactly as you know it should be done.

Experience yourself achieving your goal easily and with perfect control and know-how. Guide yourself through the whole event with perfection. See yourself being successful. Be aware of how it feels and what it looks and sounds like to succeed, to achieve your goal. Allow yourself to experience achievement and success completely and fully by seeing, hearing, and feeling it all.

Now imagine yourself warming down, relaxing, and putting on your sweats as you head for the locker room. Imagine yourself doing whatever you do after you compete or finish a major workout. Pay attention to the people around you, what they are saying and doing—anything that might be important to your visualization. Be sure to include all people or possibilities so that you will be prepared for anything that may happen in the actual competition. You may also want to think of simple key words or phrases you can recall during competition, such as "strong," "relaxed," "confident," "smooth," or "centered." While visualizing, if you reach a point in your performance when you usually have trouble or self-doubt, this is the time to use these key words or your affirmations. They will help you refocus, concentrate on your goal, and let go of any distractions or negative energy.

When you are finished with your visualization, bring your attention back to your breathing and slowly begin to come back to your body and the space you are in. Remember your feelings of confidence, fitness, and mental toughness; remember those feelings of success and achievement. You can recall these images and feelings any time you choose. You may notice that your position has changed, that your breathing is different than when you started, that you feel tired, or that you feel as if you have all new energy. These changes are due to the power of the visualization you have just experienced.

Visualizing on the day of competition may not be beneficial for some athletes. It may cause them to lose their focus, or it may cause them to get too "hyped up" and therefore lose control. It may also cause them to relax too much and not be sharp enough for their peak performance. For example, four young men, members of a 400-meter relay team, were headed from New York to New Jersey on the subway to compete in a track meet. As they stood hanging onto the straps, one of them suggested that each man visualize his leg of the relay using a stopwatch for timing. Their goal would be to run each leg as close to 10 seconds as possible. As they traveled, hanging onto the straps, they visualized each leg over and over, each runner performing to his peak. They reached the track and competed and finished dead last. When they discussed the race, they found that they were all so exhausted from having run their legs so many times between New York and New Jersey that they were too tired to run well in the actual competition!

With that being said, for most athletes, visualizing works best during the week or weeks leading up to a specific competition. It is most effective when used at least once a day at a time when you are relaxed and undisturbed for at least 20 minutes, such as right before you fall asleep at night. On the other hand, this may be the worst time if visualizing excites and energizes you.

Writing a Visualization

Teaching yourself how to visualize will help you to do automatic visualizations in the future. They will become second nature to you. Table 6.1 lists 10 steps you can follow to write your own visualization script. Refer to these steps as you write out your visualization script using Mental Trainer #8.

Reread your visualization and make sure the first part includes the start of your competition, which means warming up, stretching, awareness of the competition area, the crowd, and the environment in general. The beginning of the visualization should also include focusing on your goal and the outcome you wish to achieve. It should include everything important up to the moment you begin to physically compete—the gun sounds, the game begins, the clock starts.

The middle part of the visualization should consist of the event itself: every move you make, all your strategy, everything up to and including the finish—the finish line, the final buzzer, or the end of your routine. All the thoughts, feelings, physical moves, pains, sounds, and reactions should be included.

The final part encompasses all that happens after you have competed. This may include the shouts of the crowd, your warm-down, your victory lap, your reaction to yourself and those around you, any award you receive, joining your team, and leaving the competition area. This part also includes the reconnection with your body and the space you are in—the chair you sit in or the floor you lie on, the sounds around you, your present reality.

Be sure you have included as many senses as you can and have given yourself time to see, hear, or feel each thing you think is important to this visualization. Take your time to enjoy, to learn, to experience each movement and moment. See it all perfectly

Table 6.1   10 Steps to Writing Your Own Visualization

1. See, hear, and feel yourself performing your event.

2. Write down and dictate into a recorder every detail you can see, hear, and feel.

3. Begin with arriving at the event, going through your normal preparatory routine, and the few minutes before you perform.

4. Go into vivid detail about the event and your experience of it, including sounds, colors, smells, the crowd, the weather, the positive feelings in your body, and your mental state.

5. Imagine yourself being totally relaxed, confident, powerful, and in complete control of your body and mind. Include your affirmations and key words that will help you during your real performance.

6. Go through your whole event thinking of each significant point or play. Feel yourself moving smoothly and performing with strength and endurance.

7. After writing your visualization, write statements of relaxation, and remind yourself of your confidence, power, and mental toughness.

8. Now write your visualization in script form. Reread it and edit it. Then dictate it yourself or have someone else dictate it into your recorder.

9. Listen to the recorded visualization for flaws and make changes to the script. When you are satisfied with the script, dictate a progressive relaxation section that you feel will relax you most effectively before the visualization. Then dictate your finished script so that it follows the relaxation section.

10. Listen to the finished tape once a day or at least three or four times a week before an event. Pick a quiet time and place where you won't be disturbed. Morning or night is usually a good time. Try to stay awake to get the full effect. Sitting up is helpful. It is best to be relaxed and aware. Please do not listen to it while you are driving a motor vehicle.

and as completely as you know how. Experience it exactly as you want it to be in reality.

Once you write your own visualization, read it and make corrections. Next, read it slowly into your recorder, or have a friend record it for you. Listen to it for speed and pace. If it is too slow or too fast, record it again and listen again. Keep redoing it until you feel it is the right one for you. When you get the recording you want, listen to it as often as you want. Focus on your words, actions, and images, knowing that this personal visualization will improve your concentration and focus, and will assist you in positive mental preparation.

Mental Trainer #8:   Fine-Tuning Your Visualization

Break your visualization into three basic parts: the beginning—before you compete; the middle—your competition; and the end—your victory lap, warm-down, and return to the locker room. The beginning of the visualization should always be preceded by progressive relaxation, centering, and letting go of your physical connections.

Goals:

Affirmations and key words:

Visualization:

Visualizing As an Individual

These visualizations focus on your individual viewpoint as an athlete. They represent the different situations where an individual athlete may need to visualize. These visualizations are different from those for a team because they focus on the point of view of the person performing. You can move directly into any of the visualizations that seem important to you and to your development of a peak performance program. You should have enough information to go directly to the visualization that works best for you. Read each one and pick the one or two that seem right for you.

Visualization for Goal Achievement

Let go of your body and time completely and begin to think of a time in your life when you knew that you knew . . . a time when you were "right on" and performed perfectly. See yourself at that time . . . notice what you look like, what you are wearing, who is with you, what sounds are around you, where you are . . . feel the environment and the energy. Begin to see yourself doing whatever it was you did when you knew you were right on . . . when everything worked perfectly . . . when you were in complete control and at your peak. Watch yourself and feel that feeling . . . connect with all the feelings you experienced as you achieved at your highest level . . . perfectly . . . competently . . . exactly the way you wanted to . . . what did it feel like? . . . sound like? . . . look like? Let it all come back to you . . . let it in . . . know it again . . . the joy . . . the power . . . the pride and confidence . . . the completeness . . . the rush of knowing you were perfection . . . let it become part of you . . . part of your spirit . . . part of your being. Feel fully connected with it all.

Now, while completely involved with this absolute knowing, give yourself a word or short phrase that brings all these feelings, pictures, and sounds sharply into focus . . . a word or phrase that completely connects you with that time and those feelings when you knew that you knew . . . that you were perfect and right on . . . say the word or words to yourself several times . . . slowly . . . and allow yourself to experience your sense of power and wholeness . . . feel it in your whole body.

Think of your goal . . . what you want to achieve . . . the importance it has for you . . . remember how it felt to write it down and see it on paper. Begin to see yourself preparing to achieve this goal. Where are you and what do you look like? Are there other people there to assist you? What are they saying? Begin to go for your goal . . . see and feel yourself starting . . . moving toward your personal fulfillment. Give yourself permission to have it just the way you want it to be . . . see it perfectly as you move closer and closer to your goal . . . feel that excitement and rush that comes with doing something well, flawlessly, and with control . . . connect with your excellence as you reach and attain this important goal . . . let yourself have it, feel it, see it, know it completely . . . say your special word or phrase . . . know those feelings . . .

that power . . . see your peak performance . . . exactly the way you want it to be.

Know that anytime you need it you can call up these feelings of perfection, competence, and power simply by saying your word or phrase . . . simply by reconnecting with your inner knowing and by seeing yourself at the moment of your peak performance.

Experience yourself doing whatever you want to do now that you have reached your goal . . . be aware of how it feels to achieve . . . listen to the congratulations and hear the response of the world around you . . . allow yourself to experience the full impact of the outcome . . . the result of achieving your goal . . . let it in . . . relish it . . . touch it . . . let it be . . . have it all.

Begin to let go of the image now . . . see it floating away from you . . . let it go . . . come inside to the peace of knowing and the quiet of your breathing . . . know that you have achieved at your highest level . . . you have succeeded . . . you have done it perfectly, just the way you wanted to . . . and breathe in deeply . . . bringing in new energy and peace . . . and . . . exhale slowly . . . releasing tiredness and tenseness . . . breathe . . . slowly . . . breathe.

Slowly reconnect with the chair you are sitting in or the floor you are lying on . . . move your toes . . . come back to your body . . . move your hands and fingers . . . and, quietly and gently, open your eyes.

Visualization for Power Flow

Close your eyes, focus deep down inside yourself; feel the relaxation starting at the top of your head; all through your body . . . feeling your whole body relaxed . . . take a deep breath . . . let it out . . . feel the warmth and relaxation spreading all over your body.

As you are sitting in the chair or lying on the couch . . . imagine roots going from your spine and the soles of your feet deep into the ground through the foundation of the building . . . going deep into the earth and connecting with the earth's energy . . . its strength and its power . . . its nurturing . . . and feel the energy of the earth coming up into your body . . . filling you with power and strength . . . nurturing you, healing you, connecting you.

Begin to turn your mind to a time when you felt powerful and you were in control . . . when you felt you were on . . . take a moment to remember and think of that time . . . that time of inner strength . . . when you felt powerful and in control . . . a time when you were within yourself . . . centered and connected . . . saying what you thought . . . clearly, concisely . . . you were thinking and speaking with your heart . . . let that time come back to you . . . the scene, the words, the feelings . . . when you were connected . . . clear, centered . . . a time of crystal clarity . . . perhaps a time in a meeting . . . being assertive . . . when you were talking with someone . . . when you were presenting an idea . . . maybe simply talking and sharing with a close friend or your parent . . . let the memory of that time come back into your mind . . . and imagine yourself in that situation . . . seeing the environment you were in . . . hearing the sounds . . . feeling the feelings in your body . . . a time of power, strength, flexibility, and clarity . . . allow yourself to relive that moment . . . the feelings, the sounds, the picture . . . with that clarity in mind . . . that centered and focused feeling of power and energy . . . allow yourself to think of a word that represents that state of mind . . . that state of being . . . say the word to yourself . . . feeling the feelings in your body of that experience . . . of clarity and focus and control . . . a state of inner harmony . . . that power, that flexibility.

Imagine seeing that word on a big poster somewhere in your home . . . in any colors you want . . . smiling to yourself . . . knowing when you say that word . . . or hear it . . . or see it . . . you can bring back those images and those feelings of clarity, purpose, and focus. Look at that poster on your wall, say the word to yourself, feeling the feelings in your body . . . and look at your hand in your mind's eye, noticing a small, plastic card in it, about the size of a driver's license or credit card . . . it is an exact image of that poster . . . with all the colors and your word printed on it . . . carefully turn it over to see your face on the other side . . . a very good picture of yourself . . . and seeing your name embossed underneath the picture . . . liking it . . . again turning the card over and seeing your poster on the other side . . . in all the colors, crystal clear.

Take this card and put it in a very safe place . . . knowing you can take it out at any time . . . keeping it in a place where it's safe and secure . . . remembering you have everything within you to be, to do, and to have what you want . . . saying the word to yourself again . . . and feeling the feelings in your body again . . . knowing those positive feelings are always with you.

Slowly begin to let those images fade away . . . and begin to think of what is coming up for you in the next two weeks to a month . . . whatever life events are coming up for you . . . begin to imagine yourself entering into those events and experiences with openness, flexibility, and clarity . . . seeing them as opportunities for growth and change . . . and learning . . . imagine yourself approaching them with excitement and enthusiasm . . . knowing you have your word to help you and to guide you during those times . . . your word . . . to bring back that state of focus and clarity, of being centered, and of power . . . enabling you to achieve whatever it is you want to achieve . . . see yourself going through the next month, achieving your goal with grace, power, and flexibility . . . being adaptable, open, focused, and clear . . . with style and grace . . . with inner harmony . . . reminding yourself to think with your heart . . . and to come from a place of inner balance and harmony . . . feeling peaceful inside and outside . . . a place of peace, tranquility, and clarity.

Slowly let the image fade, coming back to your body sitting in the chair or lying down . . . feeling yourself connected with the earth . . . with its nurturing and its power . . . imagining your roots coming back into the bottoms of your feet and the base of your spine . . . still feeling the nurturing power of the earth . . . connecting you . . . centering you . . . providing you with energy and power . . . on a count of three you can open your eyes, feeling relaxed and energized for the rest of the day or evening . . . one . . . move your hands and your feet . . . stretching your back and neck . . . taking a deep breath . . . letting it out . . . two . . . stretching, breathing . . . and three . . . open your eyes when you are ready . . . feeling relaxed, peaceful, and alert.

Visualization for Tennis

Imagine yourself as you arrive at the tennis courts . . . see people playing . . . feel the air, the environment . . . hear the sounds of balls and rackets . . . feel the weather on your body . . . enjoy anticipating the match . . . experience the feeling in your stomach and in your body . . . you are a little nervous, but very ready . . . remembering that these are common feelings before you play a match and that they motivate you . . .

You begin to hit on the court . . . hitting with long, powerful strokes . . . hitting smoothly . . . rapidly . . . accurately . . . feeling relaxed and confident . . . remembering some of your affirmations as you are warming up . . . "I encourage myself after a good shot . . . I am a positive person . . . I turn negative experiences into positive ones . . . I support myself . . . I am a confident player . . . I believe in myself and my abilities . . . I play each shot in the moment and I am very focused as I play . . . I am in control of my temper and I am free of anger and resentment . . . I am confident, relaxed, and play with good form . . . "

Experience yourself and the energy as you now ready yourself for the start of your match . . . you feel good and strong . . . you focus your energy and power and stand poised . . . ready for the match to begin . . .

The match starts . . . you are moving well . . . you are light and quick . . . you are focused . . . as the ball comes to you on each shot, you concentrate on the ball and you begin to establish a rhythm of bounce, hit, bounce, hit . . . hitting with power, strength, and accuracy . . . as you hit each ball, you see it going over the net exactly where you want it to go . . . you feel the perfection in your body as you hit the shot . . . you hear the sound of the ball hitting your racket in the right spot . . . notice yourself enjoying the match immensely . . . you are glad to be out on this day playing . . . and playing well . . . you feel relaxed . . . loose . . . you are breathing out as you hit each ball . . . your forehand is powerful, strong . . . accurate . . . you feel light on your feet and you are ready for each shot when it comes to you . . . you easily place the shot wherever you want it to go . . . with accuracy and ease . . .

See and feel yourself getting into position . . . the ball coming to your forehand, you are in the perfect position to hit it . . . you hit it and watch it go straight to the place on the court where you want it to go . . . you hit a forehand crosscourt, placing it well . . . the ball returns . . . you hit a backhand crosscourt . . . a forehand straight down the line . . . deep in the corner . . . you win the point and feel good about your game . . . a serve comes to your backhand, you stroke perfectly, hitting it down the line . . . another winner . . . another serve to you, coming to your forehand, you put a nice drop shot just over the net . . .

your opponent scrambles to get it and hits a high lob . . . you settle into position and quickly execute an overhand smash . . . you receive another serve . . . to your backhand and you execute a deep backhand crosscourt shot, you feel powerful and controlled . . . you win the game . . . a service break . . . you know you are good at playing aggressively and closing out points and games . . .

Experience your body's sensations . . . determination, relaxation, control, quickness . . . knowing that you are right on . . . if your opponent calls a shot out that you are sure is in, or accuses you of cheating, experience yourself remaining calm and centered . . . you focus your aggression and feelings into powerful and expert playing . . . you are sure of your own competence and ability to overcome any negative energy . . . you have a high level of confidence and composure . . . you are mentally tough and overcome any obstacles that confront you . . .

You breathe deeply and continue to focus on the ball . . . you hit each stroke with power, accuracy, and control . . . if you miss a shot, you notice what you did in error, make the necessary adjustments, and let it go . . . letting go easily of any negativity you might feel . . . always coming back to the present moment for the next point . . . alert and ready for whatever shot comes to you . . . all that exists in your focus is one shot at a time . . . one point at a time . . . you are living and playing in the moment . . . moment to moment . . .

Experience the power you feel each time you serve . . . you are an excellent server and in control of your body and its strength and accuracy . . . imagine yourself poised to serve . . . centered . . . confident . . . powerful . . . connect with every moment . . . the height of the ball . . . the swing of your arm . . . the sound as you hit the ball in the perfect spot and send it over the net exactly where you want it to go . . . like a bullet . . . notice how your opponent has to scramble to return your serve . . . you are powerful and in control of this game and match . . .

Imagine the entire game . . . each point . . . every movement that is important to your success and the achievement of your goals . . . you trust your body and your abilities . . . and you are having fun. Continuously experience yourself as a good and competent player . . . a player who wins . . . a player who gives everything and plays the best you know how . . . you have achieved your goals . . . you have played well and feel proud, complete . . . allow yourself to enjoy it all as you remind yourself that you have everything within you to be, do, and have what you want on the court.

Visualization for Golf

You are in the locker room of the golf course. Slowly you begin to stretch your muscles . . . they feel relaxed and ready . . . they feel strong and you let your strength reach every fiber of your muscles . . . you know that you are powerful and well trained . . . this is your sport and you can feel the excitement and challenge that helps you perform . . . you lean over to your locker and pull out your golf shoes . . . you slip your feet into your golf shoes . . . tying the laces, you think of your affirmations and key thoughts for this tournament . . . you breathe . . . you feel confident, prepared, and focused as you put on your visor . . .

As you walk out onto the putting green you are aware of the feel of the grass under your shoes and the smell in the air . . . you notice the breeze on your skin and the warmth that seems to surround you . . . it is a good day and you are glad that you are in this tournament . . . you connect with your caddie . . . he is your friend and you trust that he supports you and your playing . . . you know that he is there for you and you are happy for the help . . . together you head to the range . . . you begin to think of your goal as you stretch with your club . . . moving your body gently . . . stretching and swinging without a ball . . . you feel solid and centered . . . you know that your body works together like a well-oiled machine . . . it is smooth and powerful . . . it is well trained and flexible . . . you begin to hit a few balls connecting with the feeling and the movement . . . bringing yourself within . . . you back off and let a few good swings and solid hits go through your mind . . . remembering your key word and affirmations . . . "I belong here . . . This is my game and my course . . . I have trained enough . . . I deserve to win . . . I am confident in my game and my abilities" . . . you step back up and hit a few more . . . they feel good . . . you are comfortable, taking your time . . . breathing before each shot . . . you know this helps you settle into a good tempo . . . you go through the clubs . . . gaining confidence and strength with each swing . . . as you return to the putting green, you carry a solid feeling with you . . . your short game is good . . . you stroke a few and the roll has good overspin . . . you smile to yourself . . . you feel ready and you are looking forward to this round . . .

You go back to the locker room and think of your key word, your goals, and affirmations once more . . . carefully taking yourself through a visualization of the course, and then stretching and focusing inward . . . this is your time . . . you relax and focus . . . emptying your mind of all other thoughts except the round ahead . . . you breathe . . . center and breathe again . . . you are ready . . .

As you walk to the first tee and wait for the group in front of you, you notice the people who came to watch . . . some of them came to see you . . . others just came to watch . . . you walk over to them . . . you hear them wish you good luck . . . you return to yourself and the round ahead . . . you know how to focus and find the center of your pre-shot routine . . . you give your caddie a smile as you get your club . . . you like the feel of the club and you feel its familiar grip . . . they are on your side . . . you hear your name and your list . . . you feel good about your accomplishments . . . you are totally focused now and set into your pre-shot routine . . . slowly . . . gently . . . feeling sure and solid . . . you know you are in control of the course . . . you have done clear mental work on each hole . . . this round is yours . . . your swing is powerful and smooth . . . you have great confidence in your swing . . . it feels good and you watch as the ball sails away from you heading right where you wanted it to go . . . you are pleased and you smile . . . you know you will play the course the best way for you and that is good enough . . .

As you and your caddie walk from hole to hole you talk . . . you stay focused on the game . . . you discuss what you are doing well and where you might improve . . . you laugh and support each other . . . this helps ease the tension for you . . . this is part of the fun . . . you can hear the sound of the clubs in the bag and an occasional burst of applause in the distance . . . at each hole your swings are smooth, solid, and strong . . . you stop and breathe and think each shot through making good, clear decisions . . . taking your time . . . giving it your best effort . . . you are a professional . . . you are a strong player . . . you can feel it in your walk and the time you take for each shot . . . you are concentrating and making each shot with your best effort . . . you are into it 100 percent and it feels good . . . you let yourself indulge in *your* game . . . you are worth it and it feels good . . .

You feel the pressure with just a few holes left . . . you breathe deeply and remember your strategy . . . you love this challenge . . . you know that pressure is your friend and that you rise to the occasion . . . you stay focused and relaxed . . . saying your affirmations and continuing to take your time . . . centering yourself . . . you are playing gold now . . . watching each putt fall . . . each shot lands where you want it . . . you continue your routine . . . smooth . . . centered . . . solid . . . you are great.

Each time you make a good shot the crowd cheers . . . you let its energy wash over you . . . you are proud of yourself . . . you are doing it your way and it feels good . . .

After the last putt, everyone cheers . . . you accept the praise . . . you have earned it . . . you have played the best you know how and it was good enough to reach your goal . . . you let the good feelings flow through your body . . . you worked hard and now you let yourself feel this easy sensation . . . you let the success in . . . you are excited . . . you did it . . . and it was good enough . . . you walk off the green enjoying being finished . . . in the press tent or if you are stopped by the press you feel confident and pleased with yourself . . . the reporters like you and are interested in you . . . you enjoy telling them about you . . . you expand on questions and give them insight about who you are and what your game is all about . . . you love the attention and the feeling of success . . . you leave knowing it is *you* . . . you did it and you *are* that good . . . you belong here and you are great and enough . . . you know that you have everything within you to be, do, and have what you want.

Visualization for Running a 5K Race

Imagine yourself at the track or the course where you will be competing. You are wearing your uniform and your sweats. Your mind is on the 5000-meter race. Notice the environment, the weather, the sun, the clouds . . . whatever you can see and feel . . . notice the other runners and feel yourself being calm, confident, and relaxed . . . feeling great . . . looking forward to running . . . running your best . . . feeling fit and fast . . . loving the feeling of competing and running hard . . . starting well . . . running a good race . . . you are looking forward to your race and have a deep, calm feeling inside, knowing that you are very well prepared . . . you have been training hard, and you are ready . . .

Imagine yourself doing your normal warm-up routine . . . doing your stretches and strides . . . your whole warm-up sequence . . . after completing your warm-up, imagine taking off your sweats, doing your final stretches and strides, and lining up at the start . . . hear the starter giving you the instructions . . . you notice your opponents . . . you are feeling excited, exhilarated, yet calm in your mind . . . ready to run. You feel the adrenaline flowing in your body and you are relaxed and ready . . . your muscles are ready to go . . .

You stand at the starting line, feeling the familiar excitement that you feel before every race . . . the gun sounds and you take off . . . running and jostling for position . . . the pack continues to change and move as you run on . . . you take your time, staying relaxed and fluid . . . getting in position . . . staying with the people you want to stay with . . . being in the position you want to be in at the beginning of the race . . . someone may bump your shoulder . . . you keep your form and balance . . . watching the other people around you out of the corner of your eye . . . keeping track of where they are . . .

Your stride is smooth . . . you are centered and balanced and feel comfortable . . . you are enjoying this race very much . . . you love the feeling of competition and feel the power and energy surging through your body as you continue to run effortlessly . . . you feel yourself floating along easily in complete control . . .

Your mind is on your race . . . your form . . . the runners around you . . . you speed along, feeling strong and powerful, enjoying the race . . . you hear your first-mile time . . . so quickly the mile comes up . . . you are right on schedule . . . you begin to push a little harder . . . knowing this second mile is important . . . focusing on your form, your technique, your breathing . . . you begin to surge . . . passing a few people, getting into better position . . . surging, passing, keeping in contact with the pack if there is one . . .

You pass the two-mile mark . . . hearing your time . . . you adjust accordingly . . . according to your plan and strategy . . . you feel your legs under you pumping powerfully, using your arms now as you pump and begin to slowly pick up your pace . . . knowing this is an important mile . . . keeping your focus and concentration . . . surging, passing . . . thanking your body for its strength, power, and ability . . . thanking your lungs for feeding your arms and legs with oxygen . . . you run on . . . enjoying and savoring this part of the race . . . enjoying the competition . . . relaxing your jaw and your upper body . . . breathing deeply into your abdomen . . . your stride long and sure . . . you begin to pick it up again, the last 800 . . . reaching down deep inside yourself for the rest of your reserve . . . into another gear . . . you are to the last 400, and you really begin to kick hard . . . telling yourself what a great kick you have . . . passing more people . . . kicking . . . relaxing . . . driving to the finish . . . you sprint through the finish line . . . hearing the cheers of the crowd . . . feeling the joy and exhilaration of winning . . . of running a P.R. . . . you slow, catching your breath, your sides heaving . . . ah . . . air . . . you begin to jog slowly . . . hearing the congratulations of your teammates and your friends . . . you thank your body for everything it has given you . . . promising to be nice to it, and to let it rest soon . . . you have achieved your goal.

Visualizing As a Team

Though most of the visualizations described in this book are from the perspective of the individual athlete, visualizations for team players may be quite similar. Even in a team setting where there are more variables that can change, each team member has a series of tasks to do, just like the athlete in an individual sport. The moves the athlete makes may be different, but the psychological state of mind is similar, and that is what the athlete wants to change with the visualization process. The visualization for team building is for team members who want to improve their contribution to team cohesion and, therefore, to the team's performance as a whole. As part of a mental training program for a team, team members should also fill out the Affirmations for Being a Team Player and Building a Team worksheets on pages 83 and 84.

Visualization for Team Building

Begin to think of a time when you and the team were playing in a big match or in practice . . . when you were all working well together . . . like a well-oiled machine . . . everyone was playing their position with intensity, power, focus . . . playing hard and yet relaxed . . . imagine seeing and hearing your teammates playing, connecting, perfectly in sync . . . you are all superior athletes, contributing to a higher purpose of creating a unity and a team cohesion that is exciting and exhilarating. All of you working hard . . . sharing with each other . . . supreme cooperation and support . . . giving and receiving support and friendship . . . feeling the mutual support of each other's well-being and happiness . . . sharing the pain and hard work as well as the triumphs.

You know each other so well . . . feeling your own and your teammates' commitment to excellence, to playing as well as you can in every game . . . all of you easily letting go of the petty anger and resentments that come up when people spend a lot of time together . . . you easily forgive each other for these little arguments or disagreements . . . they mean nothing in the larger scheme of things . . . enjoying your friendships and being buddies . . . allow yourself to enjoy the unity and productivity of your mutual effort . . . being happy when another succeeds . . . being a team player . . . feel the feelings in your own body as you play your position, feeling powerful, in control . . . a valuable and contributing member of this winning machine . . . feel the pride you have in yourself and as part of this team . . . knowing you belong here . . . knowing when one of you wins, you all win . . . being part of a larger and more important whole . . . enjoying these moments of your life . . . moment by moment . . . experience by experience . . . all creating a more unique and interesting you . . . as a separate and important being . . . as well as part of the great whole of this team.

Think of the team goals you have written . . . think of having fun when you play . . . enjoying your interaction with each other . . . believing in each other . . . being proud of your team and what you do . . . working hard together . . . trusting each other . . . enjoying your feelings of unity and being a part of a great and more powerful whole . . . knowing you can depend on these other people to help you . . . and being willing to let them depend on you . . . for friendship, support, and coming through in the clutch of a big game.

Begin to think of a word that will remind you of these feelings, these images, these sounds of teamwork and mutual commitment to peak performance . . . say the word over to yourself . . . hearing it, seeing it, feeling it in your body . . . and remind yourself that saying this word will bring back this team experience in its entirety.

Allow yourself to remember all the things your team did that worked in this great game or practice . . . what did you do that worked so well? . . . begin to list these accomplishments mentally . . . acknowledging your progress and your excellence as a team and as an individual player . . . thank your body and mind for their contributions to that peak performance . . . knowing that being part of this team is an honor and privilege for you . . . enjoying your participation, enjoying the process of playing and winning . . . enjoying your learning and accomplishments . . . and thank yourself and your teammates for a job well done. Slowly let the images fade, coming back to your body sitting in the chair or lying down . . . feeling grounded and centered . . . and ready for the rest of the day or evening.

On a count of three, you can open your eyes, feeling alert and refreshed . . . one . . . take a deep breath . . . moving your hands and feet . . . exhaling . . . two . . . stretch your neck and shoulders . . . and three . . . open your eyes when you're ready.

After opening your eyes, write down all the things you and your team did that helped you work well together.

Affirmations for Being a Team Player

Mark the five that would be most important to you if they were true.

_____ I enjoy encouraging and supporting my teammates.

_____ I am a good team player.

_____ There is enough glory for all of us.

_____ I assist and help my teammates in any way I can.

_____ When my teammate wins, I win.

_____ I am satisfied with our wins; I trust that I did my best.

_____ I believe in myself and in my teammates.

_____ I can count on my teammates to be there when I need them.

_____ We work together well as a team.

_____ We have fun playing together.

_____ We let go of a loss and look forward with fresh enthusiasm.

_____ We play one game at a time.

_____ We have fun, work hard, and stay loose.

_____ We come through in a crunch.

_____ We believe in each other and support each other.

_____ We are proud of our team.

_____ We are proud and play with intensity and focus.

_____ The pride is back.

Building a Team

1. What do I do to help us work well together as a team?

2. What do my teammates do to help us work well together as a team?

3. What are all the things we did in a peak game that helped us work well together?

4. What could we do to create team unity and cohesiveness that we're not already doing?

5. What do we need to do to improve as a team and to be more successful?

6. What can I do personally to encourage and support my teammates?

7. I think important team goals for our team should be . . .

   a.

   b.

   c.

   d.

   e.

Visualizing a Specific Team Sport

Remember that simple visualizations can change how a player thinks and feels. It's easy to begin thinking and saying positive things instead of negative things. Simple language changes can make enormous differences in performance; therefore, visualizations and affirmations can work together to create positive change.

Football

When creating a visualization for football, you should consider some of the most common issues that plague football players:

- Injury—coping mentally with injury and healing as fast as possible.
- Physical aggressiveness—being aggressive enough on the field.
- Mental toughness—playing intelligently and hard even when in pain and exhausted, and dealing with intense pressure from the opposing team or supercritical coaches.
- Resiliency—being able to take physical abuse and go out there and give 100 percent day after day on a consistent basis.
- Determination—refusing to give up when the mental and physical strain are too much.

The following information was compiled with the help of a talented University of Oregon football player. These lists will help football players target the most important issues to think about as they write visualizations for specific football positions. The lists contain words and images that players can use in their visualizations.

Offensive Lineman
Mind-set and Attitude: mean, aggressive, intense, determined, focused

Position-Specific Issues:

- Get off on the snap count, get off fast and stay low.
- Drive-blocking situations—Come off the ball hard and low, make contact, sustain your block, and drive your man downfield.

- Pass-blocking situation—Use proper technique; get in drop back position, butt low, arms straight forward and stiff; make contact and sustain your block by moving your feet to keep the pass rusher from getting past you.
- Double-team situation—Get your shoulder into the defensive lineman's hips; the two of you root him out and push him downfield, not allowing the defensive lineman to split the double-team.

Running Backs
Mind-set and Attitude: intense, aggressive, relaxed and loose, ready for anything, quick thinker

Position-Specific Issues:
- Take the handoff and hit the hole hard (keeping your legs moving, running fast); be totally aggressive, keeping your feet moving.
- Take the handoff and see the whole field; if the designated gap is closed, find your hole and go for it.
- If a defender comes up to tackle you, run over him aggressively.
- After getting by the first defenders, you're in the open field; you see the whole field, see your blockers, and make your cuts off your blockers, going all the way—a breakaway for a touchdown!
- Catching a pass—Run your pattern precisely, knowing when the ball is in the air, watching it coming straight into your hands. Once you've caught the ball and are holding it safely, turn upfield and run.
- Blocking—Attack the defender aggressively, staying low and blocking with good technique and aggression, taking the defender out of the play.

Quarterback
Mind-set and Attitude: calm, collected, relaxed, alert and ready, focused, confident, upbeat, team leader

Position-Specific Issues:
- Seeing the whole field—See all your receivers and the defenders; find your open man and execute a perfect pass; read defenses and make sight adjustments.

- Have total confidence in the offensive linemen protecting you.

- Be ready for the unexpected, or a situation where your receivers are covered; see your opportunity to run—turning upfield, seeing your offensive linemen going out to block for you, making your cuts off your blockers, and running for the first down.

- Showing leadership—You call the plays with authority, remembering you are a leader; be enthusiastic and determined, instilling confidence in other members of the offense.

I am attentive and confident.

Receiver and Tight End

Mind-set and Attitude: aggressive, confident, focused, quick in mind and body

Position-Specific Issues:

- Running precision patterns—Run your pattern with precision and perfection, beating your defender.
- Watch the ball coming into your hands, catching it and tucking it away, you turn upfield, making a quick move to get by your defender, and running upfield for a touchdown with power, strength, and speed. (Always lock the ball away before turning upfield.)
- Catching the ball across the middle—Watch the ball all the way into your hands, your concentration totally on the ball; taking your hit and holding on tightly to the ball, you get a first down.
- Blocking—Seeing your assigned man to block, on the snap of the ball, you attack the defender with power and aggression, taking him out of the play. Knockdowns.

Defensive Back

Mind-set and Attitude: focused, relaxed, loose, aggressive, confident, strong belief in self

Position-Specific Issues:

- Man-to-man defense—Find your man, use perfect technique covering your man; when you can get two hands on the ball, go for it!
- Zone defense—See all the receivers; when a receiver comes into your zone, react and cover him with perfection, denying him the pass.
- Defending a run—React to the run, attacking the running back with aggression and executing a perfect tackle; use proper leverage.
- Making an interception—See the ball in the air, react with power and quickness to the ball; watch the ball into your hands, intercept it and run upfield, using your blockers and going for a touchdown.

Defensive Lineman

Mind-set and Attitude: tough, aggressive, determined, intense, focused, persistent

Position-Specific Issues:

- React aggressively on the snap of the ball; when the offensive lineman fires out at you, keep low—pad level; use your hands to separate the offensive lineman from your body, find the ball carrier; shedding the offensive lineman, make an aggressive tackle for no gain by the running back. *Attack.*
- Rushing the passer—React on the snap of the ball; recognizing it's a pass from the offensive line position, use your hands and make a quick pass rush move on the offensive lineman, getting by him and sacking the quarterback for a loss.
- Defending the run—React on the snap of the ball; recognizing it's a run, fire into the offensive lineman; you feel and see the double-team from another offensive lineman; with aggression and quickness, you drop your body and split the double-team, creating a pile at the line of scrimmage.

Kicker

Mind-set and Attitude: calm, cool, collected, focused, relaxed, good under pressure

Position-Specific Issues:

- Kicking extra points, punts, and so on, both from the outside and from the inside of your body depending on your kicking style.
- Maintain a fairly narrow focus on the ball, goal crossbar, and your own physical power and accuracy.
- Stay simultaneously relaxed and focused.

The following visualization is a sample that can be adapted to other positions by changing some of the key words.

Visualization for Football

It is the beginning of a game . . . you have warmed up . . . stretched . . . listened to the final instructions and connected with your inner self . . . you say your word as you move onto the field, taking the correct position for this defensive play . . . you are supremely confident . . . ready and relaxed . . . you are focused . . . you love playing football and turning on your aggressiveness just when you need it. You know you will give it your best and you feel your energy and control. You can get total release and play with complete abandon and skill. You move . . . running . . . hitting hard . . . powerfully . . . you run right through your opponent on your tackles and when taking on blockers . . . experience yourself play after play . . . experience the team completing each play through the first quarter and into the second . . . each time the defense is on the field, you play well . . . powerfully . . . running . . . blocking . . . charging with complete confidence and skill . . . you are relaxed yet powerful . . . you are playing with abandon and control . . . experience it all . . . moving easily . . . powerfully . . . no fear . . . only competence . . . confidence and control.

Now the team is kicking off . . . you are on the kickoff team . . . you love playing on special teams, and you are the best player . . . this gives you energy and confidence . . . you believe in your strength and abilities. Life has been good to you, and you thank your mind, body, and spirit for their health, fitness, and energy. You are totally aggressive when you are on special teams . . . experience yourself playing just the way you want to . . . just the way you know a great player plays . . . you are that great player, and you accept your competence and success . . . play after play you do it correctly . . . powerfully and aggressively.

As the second half begins, you remember your word . . . and notice that you are relaxed and ready . . . feeling confident as you watch the offense . . . learning . . . waiting your turn . . . you imagine watching yourself each time you are on the field . . . moving . . . running . . . hitting . . . tackling . . . being in the right spot at the right time . . . every defense . . . every change of position you handle with confidence and great skill . . . you are a dominant player . . . you are a smart player . . . the best . . . and this is good . . . good for you and good for the team. Into the fourth quarter now . . . playing aggressively . . . meeting your goals . . . allowing yourself to have it all . . . playing with complete skill. You are pleased with your abilities . . . from one end of the field to the other . . . from one defensive play to another, you enjoy being successful . . . you are supreme . . . you are agile . . . quick . . . powerful and strong . . . confident and whole . . . play after play . . . experience it all . . . watch it all . . . you love the feeling of being in the middle of the action, and you trust your body and your mind to be there for you . . . you are whole . . . powerful . . . quick . . . relaxed . . . strong and victorious . . . allow yourself to hold on to the feelings of success . . . it makes you complete . . .

knowing what a powerful player you are . . . what a confident player you are and how important your role is to the team . . . again remembering your word . . . and that you have everything within you to be, to do, and to have what you want . . . you are your own greatest resource.

Let the picture fade . . . knowing you will play well, game after game . . . you will always give it your best . . . you will run fast and powerfully . . . hit and tackle with complete abandon and control. Let the picture go until your mind is at peace and quiet . . . begin to focus on your breathing . . . you feel relaxed, refreshed . . . strong and confident . . . complete. Begin to reconnect with your body and your present space now . . . breathe deeply . . . exhale . . . breathe.

On a count of three, you may open your eyes . . . one . . . move your fingers and toes . . . reconnecting with your body and the sounds of the room . . . two . . . move your head and shoulders . . . focusing on your breathing . . . feeling refreshed and relaxed . . . three . . . you may open your eyes when you are ready.

Basketball

This information for the different positions in basketball was compiled by a shooting guard on the University of Oregon women's basketball team. Players can use these items as they write personal visualizations for their positions.

Point Guard

- See the whole court. Concentrate on your peripheral vision—no tunnel vision.

- Dribble with your head up.

- Protect the ball. Keep your body, arm, or hand between the ball and the opposing defensive player.

- Play smart. As point guard, you are the team leader and need to be able to exemplify leadership qualities. Don't make mental mistakes. A positive and upbeat attitude helps the team stay motivated.

Shooting Guard

- Square up and be in triple-threat position when you receive the ball.

- Follow your shot! Keep moving toward the basket for a possible rebound.
- V-cut to get open.
- Go toward the pass—want the ball.

Post or Center

- Move a lot to get good position at all times—to receive a pass, to get in rebounding position, or just to remain a threat.
- Take the ball up strong, using power layups. Be aggressive, intimidating, and powerful.
- Pump fake to get the defensive player in the air and off balance. (This move may be appropriate to all positions.)
- Hook the defensive player to get open.

Defense

- Be in your defensive stance at all times—stay low, in a squatting position with your palms up.
- Have happy feet—stay on the tips of your toes and be ready.
- Respect the player's first step. Be wary, ready to react.
- Play smart. No reaching—move to get defensive position, don't reach.
- Deny the passing lane.
- Block out the offensive player after a shot has been put up, and then go to the boards.

This is an example of a player on the team doing a general visualization for basketball, rather than for a specific position.

Visualization for Basketball

Begin to think of a time on your home court . . . perhaps when you were having a scrimmage or just playing . . . and begin to remember that old confidence and power you felt in the past . . . as you played really well . . . feeling good, playing hard, but without effort . . . when your playing just flowed . . . easily and without effort . . . playing hard and feeling relaxed and easy in your body . . . remember that feeling of control and confidence . . . of being on top of your game . . . see yourself and imagine yourself being the excellent player that you are . . . knowing you belong here . . . feeling good about what you are doing and how you are playing . . . knowing deep down inside that you deserve to be on this team . . . that you are an outstanding player . . . feel yourself looking, playing, and feeling confident and relaxed . . . imagine the coaches being there, and you're feeling really confident and calm and comfortable being watched . . . you are proud, powerful, and in control.

Imagine yourself shooting with your elbows in and following through the way you want to . . . in great form . . . you are focused and centered on the play, and you know you are paying attention to the action in the game . . . you know what's happening all the time . . . you are aware and alert, ready for anything that happens . . . the crowd's noise is in the background . . . it excites you . . . you get energy from it . . . and you are focused on the game and the action . . . you are playing . . . and you are concentrating well . . . with intensity and power . . . you are enjoying yourself immensely . . . if you make a mistake, you quickly let go of it . . . putting your concentration and focus on the game . . . letting go easily and going on.

You are quick and strong, and you really enjoy being in the game, doing everything the way you want to do it . . . you are consistent in your shooting . . . shooting strong and accurately . . . seeing the ball go through the hoop . . . you are shooting well and handling the ball well, moving fast yet relaxed, and playing with intensity and focus . . . looking around, either shooting or passing it off with power and control.

Feeling those feelings of power, confidence, and control surge through your body . . . playing hard and intensely . . . with a certain relaxation of mind and body . . . that state of being . . . saying your word to yourself to bring up those feelings of power, accuracy, and confidence . . . remembering that your word connects you with that state of mind and state of being, of excellence and peak performance . . . feeling it in your mind and body . . . knowing you have what you need.

In that same gym or on any court, imagine yourself now in a big-game situation . . . an important game . . . knowing it's okay to feel a little nervous . . . and knowing that it's a natural thing . . . tell yourself, "It's okay that I'm a little nervous . . . it helps me get psyched up . . . I let go of worry easily . . . I'm powerful and aggressive . . . " See yourself and feel yourself being very intimidating . . . you *are* intimidating . . . you are big and strong . . . and you are intimidating . . . feel yourself being aggressive . . . and know you are making your opponents work to keep up with you . . . imagine yourself getting that ball . . . and if you see an opening, passing it off . . . and if you see an opportunity to shoot, going for it . . . making that commitment to shoot . . . and just doing it . . . following through . . . without hesitation . . . in an instant, stopping, looking, choosing your move and committing to an action . . . whatever it is, whether passing the ball off or shooting it yourself, you are doing it right . . . you are in charge . . . you get the ball back . . . and you are in charge . . . you let go of any worry about what people are thinking about you . . . you don't care . . . all you care about is getting the ball and playing with focus and intensity . . . telling yourself, "I'm focused on the game, and I'm having fun and I am enjoying it all . . . I'm a good player in the crunch . . . and a good team player . . . I support the whole team . . . we all help each other . . . I get better and better with each game . . . I am more and more relaxed with each passing day." Allow yourself to experience it fully, knowing you can call up this total experience any time you choose.

Slowly let the images fade . . . and become aware of your body sitting in the chair or lying on the couch . . . know that with every scrimmage and game you are going to get stronger and stronger . . . and more confident . . . on a count of three, you may open your eyes . . . feeling relaxed, refreshed, and ready for the rest of the day . . . one . . . move your hands and feet, taking a deep breath . . . and letting it out with a sigh . . . two . . . move your neck and shoulders, stretching . . . and three . . . open your eyes when you are ready.

Soccer

A college soccer coach suggested the following list of items and the general soccer visualization. They are not specific to any one position on a soccer team.

Here are the items to include when you create a soccer visualization:

- Use good body form—good balance and body position on trapping.
- Keep up your intensity (staying awake and alert—no lapses in intensity).

- Anticipate what is coming your way. Keep on your toes and be ready for what's happening. This helps you stay involved and alert.
- Take your time shooting—no rushing of shots.
- Be composed and have good form.
- Think about specific moves. Each move should become an automatic response.
- Develop your ability to recognize how you can help.
- Notice who is the most likely player to receive the pass.
- See where the space is.
- Stay in close proximity after passing off the ball.

Visualization for Soccer

Begin to remember the best soccer match you ever played . . . where it was, who was playing with you, all the sights and sounds of it . . . the excitement, the power, the achievement of your peak performance . . . allowing yourself to feel all the feelings from that time . . . of pride, confidence, achievement, excitement, fun . . . seeing the match . . . hearing all the sounds of your teammates yelling and supporting each other . . . the crowd and its cheering and clapping . . . remember it all . . . and begin to think of a word that represents that state of mind and that state of being . . . to represent all those feelings of confidence, pride, excitement, achievement . . . saying the word over to yourself . . . knowing your word will bring that time back to you whenever you wish . . . that time of peak performance and achievement.

Now begin to think of your next match . . . your goals and what you want to accomplish . . . how you want to play . . . what you want to do . . . knowing about the other team . . . imagining what your strategy will be . . . and what you want to accomplish personally.

Imagine yourself at the soccer field where your next match will be held . . . see yourself and your teammates warming up . . . running, making your moves . . . practicing your shots . . . getting ready for your match . . . feeling the familiar feeling in your stomach . . . excitement . . . anticipation . . . really enjoying the whole process . . . and remembering your word that connects you with your previous peak performance . . . saying it over to yourself . . . bringing up your confidence in yourself and your teammates.

Imagine yourself being as aggressive as you want to be . . . getting the ball . . . looking for a pass . . . breathing deeply, running powerfully, looking, committing yourself to your move . . . being completely relaxed and poised . . . in total control . . . being fast and aggressive . . . confident . . . powerful.

And seeing yourself on the field, focusing on the player you're guarding . . . thinking about what you're going to do next . . . staying alert . . . knowing when to make your move . . . being ready . . . remembering your affirmations.

"I'm strong. I'm fast. I have good concentration and focus. I stay with the player I'm guarding. When the time is right, I go for it! I'm mentally tough." Knowing that you are intimidating . . . aggressive, powerful . . . making good shots . . . having great endurance and speed . . . using your body well—shielding . . . heading . . . good at getting it, jumping up and heading . . . having a good shot . . . concentrating really well and focusing on hitting it directly . . . hearing how it sounds when you hit the sweet spot of the ball . . . following through . . . solidly kicked and feeling good . . . seeing your fakes, your moves, your one-on-ones . . . all well done . . . with good intensity and focus . . . anticipating what is coming your way and being ready for it.

Imagine yourself collecting a pass . . . turning the ball away from a defender . . . making good contact with the ball . . . feeling in control and powerful . . . then passing to a teammate . . . seeing who to pass to . . . seeing where the space is . . . staying in close proximity after passing it off.

Know that you have everything you need to play well and at your best . . . you and your teammates play well as a team . . . supporting each other . . . yelling to each other . . . playing together as a well-oiled machine . . . enjoying the team play . . . getting better and better with each game . . . and when you are getting tired . . . reminding yourself that you are strong, powerful, and fast . . . you are as tough as anyone else on the field today . . . believing in yourself and your ability . . . knowing you are a winner.

Slowly allow the images to fade . . . remembering your word . . . your word of power and strength . . . become aware of your body sitting in the chair or lying on the couch . . . on a count of three, you can open your eyes . . . feeling refreshed, relaxed, and ready for the rest of the day or evening . . . one . . . move your hands and feet, taking a deep breath . . . letting it out with a sigh . . . two . . . stretch your neck and shoulders . . . and three . . . open your eyes when you're ready.

Volleyball

A Division I volleyball coach recommended the following list of items and the volleyball visualization. They represent a more general approach and are not position specific.

Here are the items to include when you create a volleyball visualization:

- Deal with stress before big matches—you want to be relaxed and ready.
- Get focused before practice—get mentally geared up before practice to get the most out of it.
- Keep calm and ready to receive the serve.
- Deal with your "Jekyll-and-Hyde" attitude—being explosive one minute and playing with a soft touch the next.
- Be flexible, with a multitude of different attitudes during the match. For blocking, be intimidating, aggressive, and powerful. For passing and setting, be loose, relaxed, and narrowly focused.
- During a match, focus on the here and now. Be present, and let go of missed points.

Visualization for Volleyball

Settle down into yourself, putting your focus inside your body . . . begin to exhale and inhale . . . breathing slowly and rhythmically . . . breathing in . . . breathing out . . . breathing in relaxation . . . breathing out tension . . . begin to think of a time in your home gym . . . perhaps when you were having a scrimmage or just playing . . . and begin to remember that old confidence and power you felt in the past . . . when you played really well . . . feeling good, playing hard, but without effort . . . when your playing just flowed . . . easily and without effort . . . playing hard and feeling relaxed and easy in your body . . . remember that feeling of control and confidence . . . of being on top of your game . . . see yourself and imagine yourself being the excellent player that you are . . . knowing that you belong here . . . feeling good about what you are doing and how you are playing . . . knowing deep down inside that you deserve to be on this team . . . and you are an outstanding player . . . feel yourself looking, playing, and feeling confident and relaxed . . . imagine the coaches being there and you're feeling really confident and calm and comfortable being watched . . . you are proud, powerful, and in control.

Imagine yourself playing . . . in good form . . . you are focused and centered on the play and you know you are paying attention to the action in the game . . . you know what's happening all the time . . . you are aware and alert, ready for anything that happens . . . the crowd's noise is in the background . . . it excites you . . . you take energy from it . . . and you are focused on the game and the action . . . you are playing . . . and you are concentrating well . . . with intensity and power . . . you are enjoying yourself immensely . . . if you make a mistake, you quickly let go of it . . . putting your concentration and focus on the game . . . letting go easily and going on . . .

You are quick and strong and you really enjoy being in the game, doing everything the way you want to do it . . . you are consistent in your shots . . . hitting strong and accurately . . . seeing the ball go right where you want it to go . . . you have great reaction time . . . and when the ball comes to you, you take your time . . . you relax and play with intensity and focus . . . looking around, placing it well and accurately.

Feel all those feelings of power, confidence, and control surge through your body . . . playing hard and intensely . . . with a certain relaxation of mind and body . . . flowing with the play . . . think of a word to represent this state of mind and this state of being . . . saying your word to yourself to bring up those feelings of power, accuracy, and confidence . . . remembering that your word connects you with that state of mind and state of being, of excellence and peak performance . . . feeling it in your mind and body . . . knowing that you have what you need . . .

In that same gym, imagine yourself now in a big-game situation . . . an important game . . . knowing it's okay to feel a little nervous . . . and knowing that's a natural thing . . . tell yourself, "It's okay that I'm a little nervous . . . it helps me get psyched up . . . I let go of worry easily . . . I'm powerful and aggressive . . . "

See yourself being very intimidating . . . you are intimidating . . . you are big and strong . . . and you are intimidating . . . feel yourself being aggressive . . . imagine the ball coming to you . . . and if you see an opening, then going for that spot . . . and just do it . . . following through . . . without hesitancy . . . taking your time . . . in an instant, stopping, looking, choosing your move, and committing to an action . . . whatever it is, you are doing it right . . . you are in charge . . . you let go of any worry about what people are thinking about you . . . you don't care . . . all you care about is getting the ball, and playing with focus and intensity . . . say to yourself, "I'm focused on the game, I'm having fun, and I am enjoying it all . . . I'm a good player in the crunch . . . and a good team player . . . I support the whole team . . . we all help each other . . . I get better and better with each game . . . I am more and more relaxed with each passing day . . . ," knowing and feeling that you are intimidating . . . aggressive, powerful . . . making good shots . . . having great endurance and accuracy . . . using your body well, being calm and alert, ready to receive the serve . . . having a good return . . . concentrating really well and focusing on hitting it directly, or setting it up perfectly for your teammates . . . hearing how it sounds when you hit the sweet spot of the ball . . . following through . . . solidly hit and feeling good . . . seeing your moves, all well done . . . with good intensity and focus . . . anticipating what is coming your way and being ready for it.

Imagine yourself being explosive one moment when you need to . . . and playing with a soft touch the next . . . being flexible and responding with the best response to each ball that comes to you . . . seeing and feeling yourself accelerating through the ball . . . blocking with fierce power . . . digging, relaxing, and enjoying the feeling . . . fearless and aggressive . . . your serve strong, powerful, and accurate . . . being a gunslinger.

See and feel yourself being flexible with a multitude of different attitudes during the match . . . being intimidating . . . aggressive . . . powerful . . . passing and setting . . . being loose and relaxed . . . narrowly focused . . . and if you happen to blow a shot, letting go easily and coming back to the here and now . . . playing in the present moment . . . forgiving yourself and your teammates for any missed shots . . . staying focused, aware, and present . . .

Allow yourself to experience it fully, knowing that you can call up this total experience any time you choose . . .

And begin to remember the best volleyball game you ever played . . . where it was, who was playing with you, all the sights and sounds of it . . . the excitement, the power, the achievement of your peak performance . . . allowing yourself to feel all the feelings from that time . . . of pride, confidence, achievement, excitement, fun . . . seeing the match . . . hearing all the sounds of the clapping . . . remember it all . . . and begin to think of a word that represents that state of mind and that state of being . . . to represent all those feelings of confidence, pride, excitement, achievement . . .

Now begin to think of your next game . . . your goals and what you want to accomplish . . . how you want to play . . . what you want to do . . . knowing about the other team . . . imagining what your strategy will be . . . and what you want to accomplish personally.

Imagine yourself at the place where your next game will be held . . . see yourself and your teammates warming up . . . making your moves . . . practicing your shots . . . getting ready for your match . . . feeling the familiar feeling in your stomach . . . excitement . . . anticipation . . . really enjoying the whole process . . . and remembering your word that connects you with your previous peak performance . . . saying it over to yourself . . . bringing up your confidence in yourself and your teammates.

Imagine yourself being as aggressive as you want to be . . . getting the ball . . . placing it well . . . breathing deeply, looking, committing yourself to your move . . . being completely relaxed and poised . . . in total control . . . being fast and aggressive . . . confident . . . powerful.

And imagining yourself in the game, focusing on the ball . . . thinking about what you're going to do next . . . staying alert . . . knowing when to make your move . . . being ready . . . remembering your affirmations.

Know that you have everything you need to play well and at your best . . . you and your teammates play well as a team . . . supporting each other . . . yelling to each other . . . playing together as a well-oiled machine . . . enjoying the team play . . . getting better and better with each game . . . and when you are getting tired . . . reminding yourself that you are strong, powerful, and accurate . . . you are as tough as anyone else in the game today, believing in yourself and your ability . . . knowing you are a winner.

Baseball or Softball

The following items should be addressed in a baseball or softball visualization:

- Pregame nervousness—Relaxing, focusing.
- Hitting—Keeping a clear mind, reacting to a pitch instead of guessing.
- Pitching—Being aggressive and smart; changing speeds; pitching with finesse, the right frame of mind, and confidence in yourself; being intimidating; having the flexibility to change strategy in the middle of the game and to be able to adjust when things go wrong.
- Doubleheaders or tournament play—Keeping your energy up and dealing with tiredness and exhaustion; keeping your intensity level up during the day; remembering the importance of each game; knowing the situation at all times; knowing where the next play is going to happen.
- Defense—Staying alert and being ready for anything; keeping your focus and concentration on the game; knowing the situation at all times; knowing where the next play is going to happen.

A professional baseball consultant in Arizona recommended an interesting technique for dealing with anxiety between pitches. This prepitch routine can also be used for batting and is especially helpful for players who have a lot of negative self-talk. This routine virtually eliminates negative self-talking by focusing on the patterns between each pitch.

After each pitch, the pitcher takes a few deep breaths to restore a semirelaxed state, says a cue word to himself about relaxation, such as "relax," and assumes a relaxed posture; then he begins to reflect on analyzing the next move or pitch, thinking of strategy. The pitcher then says a cue word to himself for optimal arousal and peak performance, and then pitches. These activities very effectively switch the focus from negativity to relaxation and strategy.

I am fast and accurate.

A batter can use the same pattern, relaxing between each pitch and getting ready for the next one with good concentration and focus.

Visualization for Baseball or Softball

Begin to remember the best game you ever played . . . where it was, who was playing with you, all the sights and sounds of it . . . the excitement, the power, the achievement of your peak performance . . . allowing yourself to feel all the feelings from that time . . . of pride, confidence, achievement, excitement, fun . . . seeing the game . . . the players . . . hearing all the sounds of your teammates yelling and supporting each other . . . the crowd and its cheering and clapping . . . remember it all . . . and begin to think of a word that represents that state of mind and that state of being . . . to represent all those feelings of confidence, pride, excitement, achievement . . . saying the word over to yourself . . . knowing that your word will bring that time back to you whenever you wish . . . that time of peak performance and achievement.

Now begin to think of your next game . . . your goals and what you want to accomplish . . . how you want to play . . . what you want to do . . . knowing about the other team . . . imagining what your strategy will be . . . and what you want to accomplish personally.

Imagine yourself at the field where your next game will be held . . . see yourself and your teammates warming up . . . throwing, catching, quickly moving . . . making all your moves at your particular position . . . practicing your throwing . . . your catching . . . getting ready for your game . . . feeling the familiar feeling in your stomach . . . excitement . . . anticipation . . . really enjoying the whole process of a game . . . anticipating playing hard and fast . . . and remembering your word that connects you with your previous peak performance in your best game . . . saying it over to yourself . . . bringing up your confidence in yourself and your teammates.

Imagine yourself being as aggressive as you want to be . . . getting to the ball as it comes to you . . . throwing it precisely and quickly where it needs to go . . . right in your teammate's glove . . . or catching the ball and tagging the runner perfectly . . . breathing deeply, looking, committing yourself to your move . . . being completely relaxed and poised . . . in total control . . . being fast and aggressive . . . always on the alert . . . watching . . . seeing . . . reacting . . . confidently . . . powerfully.

And seeing yourself on the field, focusing on the ball and the other players on the field . . . thinking about what you're going to do next . . . staying alert . . . knowing when to respond . . . being ready . . . remembering your affirmations.

"I'm quick. I'm fast. I throw the ball accurately. I have good concentration and focus. When the time is right, I go for it! I'm mentally tough." Knowing that you are a great player . . . aggressive, powerful . . . having a clear mind . . . being able to change speeds . . . with finesse . . . using your body well.

Imagine yourself at your position . . . the ball coming toward you . . . being right where you need to be to make the perfect play . . . your body and mind flexible and fast moving . . . feeling in control and powerful . . . then throwing to a teammate . . . seeing who to throw to . . . seeing where the play is.

Begin to think about your turn at bat . . . see yourself getting a base hit . . . or better . . . a home run . . . focusing on hitting it directly . . . keeping a short stride at bat . . . throwing your hands at the ball . . . hitting it hard . . . reacting with precision, accuracy, and power . . . hearing how it sounds when you hit the sweet spot of the ball . . . following through . . . solidly hit and feeling good . . . seeing and feeling yourself hit the ball solidly and running the bases . . . all well done . . . with good intensity and focus . . . having anticipated the pitch coming your way and having been ready for it.

Know that you have everything you need to play your best . . . you and your teammates play well as a team . . . supporting each other . . . yelling to each other . . . playing together as a well-oiled machine . . . enjoying the team play . . . getting better and better with each game . . . and when you are getting tired . . . reminding yourself that you are strong, powerful, and fast . . . you are as tough as anyone else on the field today . . . believing in yourself and your ability . . . knowing you are a winner.

Seeing Ahead

This chapter has given you all the tools you need to write your own visualizations. You can use the specific visualizations for your sport, or change them, or write something entirely new for yourself. Recording yourself saying the words of the visualization and listening to it once per day during the week before your competition is a very effective strategy. Following the steps outlined in 10 Steps to Writing Your Own Visualization (table 6.1 on page 69) will give you the best visualization for you.

Chapter 7

Optimizing Your Performance

The athletes' message is clear. The difference between best performances and worst performances lies within their thoughts.

Terry Orlick

This chapter includes techniques for focusing and refocusing, overcoming burnout, and keeping your motivation high while training hard. For peak performance, feeding the body and mind is just as important as what you think.

Focusing Attention

A key feature of mental training is the use of concentration techniques. Concentration is the process of paying attention and focusing. The better your concentration, the better athlete you can be. However, an important component of this process is the *what* of your concentration. What are you paying attention to? What is your focus? If you are paying attention to your negative self-talk, or if you are looking in the wrong direction, having lost your focus, you will play poorly. If you are focused on your technique, your breathing, your body, the ball, or the person you are guarding, you will have the opportunity to play your best. After physical techniques and training are mastered, the path to your peak performance is your mental strength.

People are often taught to multitask, doing several things at once. The ultimate goal in an athletic performance, though, is to be able to focus on one thing without letting the mind wander. This takes practice, and lots of it, because often in a game or match your focus will change from second to second. You must be conscious of your process of thinking and have the ability to change it if it is not working for you.

In a game situation, sometimes multitasking is necessary. Overall, however, the athletes who are able to be in the "zone" of total concentration are the most likely to achieve their goals. In team sports, athletes must pay attention to what is going on around them, and they must also be able to concentrate on the ball or on guarding or blocking out their opponent.

An important part of focusing comes when you have made a mistake. You must be able to regain your focus and make the best of the situation you're in. Stopping negative self-talk, forgiving yourself, and resolving to do better in the next play go a long way toward enabling you to play your best. If your teammates make a mistake, forgive them and encourage them. Most likely, they are already upset with themselves for messing up. Your encouragement can help them move forward and let go of their mistake more easily.

In either individual or team sports, when you are not competing, you can concentrate on your form by doing a visualization or imagery exercise of a particular move. You can also think of the "what-ifs" that might come up in a competition and of how you would handle those situations in a positive way. This mental work will help your body respond positively, and often automatically, if a worst-case scenario occurs.

So, then, how do you learn to focus your attention? In American culture, people are bombarded by stimuli everywhere in their environment. You may be able to study, listen to music, talk on the phone, and work on your computer all at the same time. And if you can do well in all, more power to you! However, if you do learn to focus on one thing at a time, that singular focus will help you in the long run. There are many techniques for focusing. For instance, if you are in class or in a meeting, see how long you can concentrate on what the speaker is saying without letting your mind wander. How well can you listen without thinking about what's next in your day or what you want to eat for dinner? For many people, this is a challenge.

In sports, there are two types of focus: a single-pointed focus on the "small picture" of guarding your opponent, and a double-pointed focus on the "big picture" of guarding your opponent *and* knowing what is happening around you. Each person has different ways of paying attention. However, focusing skills can be learned and mastered with practice. When your mind wanders, you'll know how to bring your attention back to the present moment!

Sometimes you may lose focus and concentration when you think about the past or think ahead to the future. While you are thinking of these other times, you are no longer present in your life. Daydreaming is great, but sometimes you need to pay total attention to your present circumstances. In these cases, you may have to refocus your concentration. The techniques for refocusing are basically the same as for focusing. Remember, you must mentally let go of distractions or mistakes, encourage yourself, and move on. You can use the following techniques to focus or refocus on the present moment.

- Listen to visualization tapes. Sit in a comfortable position; the more you can focus on what is being said, and the more you can visualize, the more you will be able to stay focused in a competition.

- Keep eye control. Notice where you are looking and make sure you are looking at the ball or the player you're guarding, depending on the situation. In running, for example, you might notice where your eyes are focused when you run your best.

- Control your mind and body. Calming words said to yourself internally can help you focus or refocus. Words such as "calm," "breathe," or "focus" can help you pay attention and direct your attention. If you notice you are feeling upset, concentrating on your breathing or on relaxing part of your body can help you regain control of your focus.

- Visualize and imagine. Visualize in short segments what you want to do in certain situations and imagine yourself doing it perfectly. Make these images brief at first so that you can keep your focus. Notice your environment in these images. These shorter visualizations are a way of keeping you in the present moment and helping your concentration and attention to detail. The idea is to be conscious of your personal process so that you can change it if you don't like it or if it isn't working for you.

- Blink your eyes. To release emotional tension and to help you refocus, rapidly blink your eyes five or six times; then squeeze your eyes shut and open them wide four or five times; then take three deep breaths, inhaling deeply through your nose and exhaling out your mouth. Move your eyes from far left to far right to balance both sides of your brain. Then refocus on what you are doing.

- Remember to breathe. If something has caused you to lose your concentration, taking a moment to consciously breathe into the solar plexus area (above your waist) or into the tan tien (two inches below your navel) will help you to re-center yourself and get you back into your body in awareness. Take a deep breath through your nostrils and visualize the breath and its energy flowing down your spine in a channel all the way into your solar plexus; on the exhale, visualize the breath and its energy flowing out of the energy center and into the air in front of you. Take three or four breaths in this manner. This will calm you, energize you, and help you refocus your attention.

- Learn to meditate. If you find it difficult to learn to focus on one thing at a time, your mind chatter may be getting the best of you. Taking a meditation class might help you learn to let go of your repetitive thought patterns. You can find classes that teach various meditation techniques in most cities and on many college campuses. Most meditation practices emphasize single-pointed focus. This can be achieved in various ways, such as mentally repeating a mantra (a word or phrase), guided meditations (which are similar to guided visualizations), or focusing on your breathing pattern and blank mind. For a person with lots of mind chatter, imagining the words as a river flowing by and just watching the river often helps stop the chatter. Letting the words go by or picking them up is a choice. Play with these techniques and see what works for you.

Overcoming Burnout

Whether you are an Olympic gold medalist or a recreational athlete, you should have fun and enjoy your sport. For some people, their work is like play; for some, it's all work and no play; and for others it's work hard, play hard. How serious do you want to be in your sport? You are probably pretty serious about it or you wouldn't be reading this book to improve your performance. You can have fun and still be serious. Most people take themselves too seriously anyway. They are afraid to lose face or to be embarrassed. Many people are afraid to lose because they think they will be seen as a loser. But the judgment begins within yourself. Most other people aren't paying much attention to you; they're more self-focused, just as you are. How much attention do you pay to others? Probably, not very much. And other people are the same way. The affirmation "I give back to others the responsibility for their own opinions and judgments" can go a long way toward

I can block and smash powerfully.

© Empics

helping you let go of your fear of being judged—your fear of being rejected because you don't measure up. Who are the omnipresent "they" anyway?

I've worked with several college athletes to help improve their motivation and mental abilities. Many were totally burned out because they started so young. They were going through the motions because they were on scholarship and needed their scholarship to pay for school. These athletes had lost their love of the game. To them, their sport was drudgery. If you have lost your love for your sport, I would advise taking some time off, staying in shape, and then returning to it six months to a year later. I started playing tennis at age 10, and I played varsity in high school and college. And then I was done. I couldn't stand playing after that. Although I still hit a few balls occasionally, my heart's not in it. I didn't start seriously running until I was 36, and then I ran marathons, 10Ks, and 1500-meter races. I still love running, but I don't compete anymore. It's not fun anymore for me to compete, so I don't do it.

Take some time to think about why you play your sport. You may play hard and train hard, and if you enjoy it, keep doing it. People need new challenges for their bodies, minds, and spirits. When I taught gerontology courses at the University of Oregon, I had "consultants" from the community paired with the students in my Psychology of Aging class. I taught this class for eight years, and every year a small group of the same consultants would return. I once asked them why they kept coming back. One said, "I may not agree with what the students are saying and doing, but I want to know what it is!" You, too, must find what gives you motivation and joy as you perform in sports and in life. May we all follow the example of this consultant and have the vigor and energy for life as it comes.

Overcoming mental and physical fatigue can be a big problem when you are training hard day after day and year after year. Mental fatigue, mental exhaustion, and distractions are a part of professional athletics and college sports. Finding a balance between enough rest and overtraining can be a real challenge. I've seen so many athletes, especially distance runners, who train so hard that they can't perform at their best in their competitions. They run a hard workout two days before a meet and then wonder why their legs are dead in the race. Overpreparation often creates mental and physical tiredness. Overanalyzing also can be a problem. Remember the old cliche, "Don't work harder, work smarter." The training base that serious athletes build for themselves can see them through small injuries and short periods without training. But many athletes panic when they can't train and think their whole career is going down the drain. Not true. They may need to sharpen up after time off, but the base is still there.

Breaking Out of a Slump

Slumps are periods dreaded by athletes because their performances suddenly decline with no apparent reason. Slumps are inevitable and frustrating, but treatable. "Slumps are repetitive performance problems that can come in several forms," explains Alan Goldberg, EdD, a private practice sport psychologist in Amherst, Massachusetts. "The one that most athletes consider a true slump is a drop in performance after a period of success. The classic example is the baseball player who hits over .300 for the first half of the season, then can't buy a base hit for the next month."

Goldberg, author of *Sports Slump Busting* (1998), says to first make sure that the problem is mental and not a technical one that needs the attention of a coach. If it is a mental problem, athletes have to understand that they have the resources to solve it. They still have control, although things seem to be out of control.

A slump is not a random event like catching the flu. No one knows where the flu came from; it's just there. Rather, slumps are caused by faulty mental mechanics that can be identified. What athletes think, say to themselves, and focus on during a slump are completely different from what they thought, said, and concentrated on when they were playing well. The trick is to be able to recognize and contrast the two thought processes.

Once athletes understand their role in the process, they must remain in control of their focus and concentration. If they don't, the outcome of competition will be determined before it begins. Negative thoughts can affect breathing, muscle tension, and other physiological responses that have a direct effect on the quality of performance.

"The whole sequence gets triggered in a negative way and the slump becomes a self-fulfilling prophesy," claims Goldberg, and he goes on to illustrate this point:

> Here's an example. A tennis player who moves to a higher level of competition looks around and sees other players hitting harder. She starts worrying that her skills are not adequate and tries to start playing a power game. Now, she's playing a style with which she is not comfortable. Contrast this to an athlete who is playing in "the zone" and is oblivious to opponents' styles or skills. (1998, *Sports Slump Busting*)

Goldberg also warns about uncontrollable factors. By paying attention to the things over which you have no control (opponents, weather conditions, playing surface, crowd noise), stress goes up,

I am in control.

confidence and performance go down. Success is more likely when athletes concentrate solely on their performance. Even better, some athletes who perform in the zone say they don't think about anything. They just play.

Don't panic if you have three or four bad performances. That happens to every athlete and does not constitute a slump. How you react to poor performances can produce the real thing. Negative thoughts can become seeds that grow into a full-blown slump.

It can take up to four to six weeks to break out of a slump. If you don't have access to a sport psychologist to help work through the problem, Goldberg suggests that you take three steps on your own: "Focus on things you can control, keep a long-term perspective on your performance, and revert to the positive mental mechanics you exhibited when you were playing well" (1998, *Breaking Out of a Slump*).

More about common performance blocks will be addressed in chapter 8 of this book, and specific techniques will be suggested to help you play your best by eliminating poor mental training habits.

Keeping Motivation High

When you need help in keeping your motivation high, the following activities may give you some new ideas on staying fresh in mind, body, and spirit.

- Get enough sleep. A few years back, a study was conducted on long-distance runners and sleep. It was discovered that the runners recovered and performed at higher levels when they got at least eight hours of sleep per night. All that hard physical training takes a toll on the body and mind. The body needs time to recover and rebuild muscle tissue.

- Do cross-training. Depending on the sport, cross-training can be helpful in keeping boredom and burnout away. One or two rest days per week, or two very light workout days, can do wonders for keeping the body happy and will contribute to your mental and physical well-being.

- Spend time in nature. Spending time in nature, whether in an urban park, a wilderness area, or your own backyard, can also contribute to an internal quietness. Inner peace is not just a mental construct. The earth has an electromagnetic energy field that soothes your body and spirit if you slow down enough to let it do its healing work. All you have to do is sit or lie in the grass. People are earth creatures but they tend to lose touch with the earth herself. Napping, reading a book, or just lying down in the grass can help rest your body and tune your body to the earth's rhythms. One of my favorite pastimes is to hike in the Cascades near my home, or the nearby Mt. Pisgah trail. Even getting away for just an hour refreshes my whole body and mind. And the silence, peace, and tranquillity from nature stay with me for several days afterward. I come back refreshed and ready to work hard again.

- Learn to meditate. Tiger Woods learned to meditate when he was a young boy and his mother took him to a Buddhist temple. While there, he spent time praying with Zen masters and learned to put himself into a state of deep concentration. Tiger subscribes to the mind, body, and spirit philosophy of peak performance. He is a master of imagery and visualization, and his focus and concentration skills are far superior to other players on the PGA tour. Captain Jay Brunza, a navy clinical psychologist, taught Tiger how to play in the zone in a round of golf. Brunza caddied for Tiger for 39 matches, of which Tiger won 33. A book by John Andrisani, *Think Like Tiger* (2002), is a good read, and for golfers, it is a treasure trove of mental training techniques for playing better golf. Other athletes can use the same techniques for their sports.

When it comes to overpreparation and overtraining, even Tiger Woods is susceptible. In the book, Andrisani describes Tiger's performances during the last three majors of the 2001 season, where he performed poorly. After winning four major championships in a row, Tiger was most likely totally burned out and physically and mentally fatigued. He then overprepared and burned himself out even more. Sometimes more is not always better. Tiger made mistakes that the common golfer makes. Andrisani says:

> Regardless of Tiger's poor play, by his standards anyway, he did not get down on himself. Like a true champion, Tiger drew strength from his disappointments, knowing he had experienced these same problems before and corrected them.

Tiger Woods, master of playing in the "zone," recovers easily from mistakes and distractions.

© Joe Robbins

That's the secret to improved play: staying positive in the face of adversity and knowing you can recover your lost game by first getting some rest, then recalling proven mental buzz phrases and working on practice drills. (2002)

This is great advice for athletes at any level.

- Listen to music, do yoga, or watch athletic videos. Keeping motivation high can be as simple as listening to music, doing yoga, or watching videos. Music can relax you, motivate you, empower you, or lull you to sleep. Many athletes listen to a favorite upbeat song before their competition to fire themselves up. Yoga of any type is a great way to stretch your body and quiet your mind, and it gives your body, mind, and spirit time to relax and let go. The flexibility required is great for the body and makes your mind more flexible as well. Videos of a season's highlights for a team, or for individual players, can be a great motivating tool that inspires a desire to play at your best. In addition, you can see proper form and techniques that create mental images in your brain as if you had done the techniques physically. Watching videos of past peak performances acts as a mental imagery reinforcer. Try not to watch videos with mistakes more than once or twice because you can also mentally reinforce these poor techniques.

- Learn new energy psychology techniques. There is a new and growing field of psychology called energy psychology, which employs a number of techniques based on tapping different parts of the body to release trauma or negative emotions. The Emotional Freedom Technique (EFT) is one of these techniques. Energy therapies are a radical departure from traditional medicine and therapeutic techniques. (For more detailed information, go to www.emofree.com. You can explore these techniques by using a search engine and typing in "energy therapy," "energy psychology," or "energy medicine.") The EFT method consists of lightly tapping at the brow point, the sides of the eyes, under the eyes, the upper and lower lips, the collarbone areas, the armpits, and points on the hands. This is done in combination with breathing and sometimes saying phrases of release such as, "Even though I have this remaining_____(problem/issue), I deeply and profoundly love, accept, and respect myself." Although this method sounds very unusual, it has had powerful effects on changing negative states of mind.

- I use EFT often with my clients for all sorts of issues and emotional upsets. In addition, I have used a technique called Rapid Eye Technology (RET) in my practice since 1994. This technique is based on accessing and reorganizing negative emotional material in the visual, auditory, and kinesthetic (body feelings) areas of the client. Every time the client goes into a sleep state, rapid eye movement occurs, a sleep cycle that is vital to feeling rested and revitalized after a night's sleep. The RET therapist has the client blink rapidly while watching peripherally a series of wand or hand movements by the therapist. The result is that this eye blinking discharges negative emotional material that has been stored in the client's brain. The therapist also speaks phrases to bring up stored emotional material. I have used RET as a supplement to my usual array of counseling techniques and have used it with athletes. It is a powerful, efficient way to release deeply held negative core issues and beliefs. Another method, Eye Movement Desensitization and Reprocessing (EMDR), is similar to RET and is also being used by sport psychologists. RET accesses the visual, auditory, and kinesthetic modalities of emotional storage, and also has a spiritual, not religious component. For more information on RET, go to the Web site at www.rapideyetechnology.com, call 503-399-1181, or send an e-mail to the Rapid Eye Institute at RETCampus@aol.com.

All the techniques described here can help you optimize your performance and help you let go of stress and tension. Now you know *what* techniques to use. A key component of peak performance is doing and practicing what you know. You have everything that you need to be, do, and have what you want. Try these techniques and see which ones work best for you.

Feeding the Mind

Much of your mental strength and stamina is based on what you put in your body. Something as simple as getting enough water can contribute significantly to your physical endurance. This also affects your mental state. If you are dehydrated, you lose energy, wastes collect in your body, and you will often perform poorly, feeling tired and depleted. In general, a person who doesn't exercise should drink at least eight glasses of water per day. For athletes who exercise strenuously, the proper amount might be two or three times that, depending on how much the athlete sweats. I recommend that my athletes drink three glasses of water when they get up in the morning to clear out the toxins in their bodies from a night of sleep. This also helps irrigate the body systems, preparing them for the day of exercise ahead.

Eating Right

Diet and nutrition are variables that many athletes don't pay enough attention to. When competing and training at a high level, athletes just want enough calories to fill them up and give them energy. Several good books on nutrition and food for peak performance are available. Peruse the bookshelves and find what is right for you. One piece of advice: Most athletes in endurance sports don't eat enough protein. Nancy Clark, author of *Nancy Clark's Sports Nutrition Guidebook* (1997) and *The Food Guide For Marathoners* (2002), says that recreational exercisers need between 75 and 112 grams of protein per 150 pounds of body weight daily. Clark says competitive athletes need 90 to 135 grams per 150 pounds of body weight. This may seem like a lot of protein. However, the muscles, ligaments, and tendons need this protein to repair themselves. Although protein bars do help when exercising, the recommended amount of protein should be obtained through the food the athlete eats, not through protein supplements. In regular meals, high-protein foods are the best way to get quality protein into your diet. Eating some protein at every meal also helps to balance the carbohydrates and keep your blood sugar levels at a healthy equilibrium. Keeping blood sugar levels even helps your brain and body function at their best. Enough water to hydrate yourself also helps your mental and physical performance.

Athletes should also pay attention to the quality of what they ingest. It is becoming more and more important to eat pure foods that are organic and to take high-quality nutritional supplements that furnish vitamins and minerals that people may not get in their meals. American fast food is becoming more questionable in terms of quality and where it comes from (where it was grown or raised and under what circumstances). With genetically altered foods, there are even more questions. When genetically altered corn pollen came in contact with monarch butterfly larvae and was eaten by the larvae, the larvae died. What does that mean?

Most processed foods (prepackaged foods) have corn, corn syrup, tomatoes, tomato paste, and soy products added to them. Many corn, tomato, and soybean crops are genetically altered. European countries will not import certain foods from the United States that have been genetically altered. What do they know that Americans don't? Perhaps their industries aren't as influential. In truth, nobody knows any of the long-range implications of genetically altered products on the human body. People are told they are safe. In the past, people have been told other products and drugs were safe, only to find out 10 years later that they were not.

So again, be conscious of what you are eating and where it came from. You don't have to be paranoid; just be aware. Also, with dairy products, it can be a healthful choice to drink organic milk. If you eat organic dairy products, you can be sure that there are no extra hormones or steroids in the milk or beef. Naturally raised beef and chickens are better for you. Be aware that all organic produce and products are more expensive than nonorganic. This is because organic farmers cannot grow the huge amount of crops that are grown with fertilizers and pesticides. The old saying "you are what you eat" couldn't be more true than it is today. Some foods are unhealthy, and it is up to you to select healthy choices for yourself. If you don't, who will?

Avoiding Addictions

As the saying goes, "just say no." Many athletes are tempted, especially from the teens to the thirties, to use recreational drugs. In college and elite circles, the drug of choice besides alcohol is often marijuana, which is easily available. A vast number of people use marijuana regularly, even though it is an illegal drug in the United States. Almost half of young people between 18 and 30 have tried it. The effects of marijuana use are described in a research summary of the medical literature reported by Christiane Northrup, MD, in her newsletter:

> People who use marijuana daily for many years may have difficulties with learning, memory and attention. A University of Iowa study showed that heavy marijuana use (seven or more times/week for at least six years) was associated with modest but significant deficits in memory, verbal expression, and math performance.
>
> Long-term use produces lingering deficits in what is known as selective attention. Studies have shown that users can't even stay focused on subjects of interest to them. The more years they've used marijuana, the more problems they're likely to have focusing.

- Frequent marijuana use appears to decrease information-processing speed.

- Other behavior changes associated with marijuana use include apathy, aimlessness, loss of motivation to achieve, lack of long-range planning and decreased productivity.

- Smoking marijuana can cause lung damage. This can be seen after one year of daily use.

- It is known to decrease sperm counts and the level of testosterone and other reproductive hormones. It also increases the ratio of female to male hormones in the body, causing males to have breast development. (Northrup 2002)

If your family has a history of alcoholism or other addictions, it is in your own best interest to not indulge in these substances. The chemical high that is produced in the brain feels good and numbs emotional and physical pain. Please find natural ways to cope with your pain or to raise your endorphin levels. If you are a college or elite athlete, drug tests could put an end to your career. For most athletes, the risk is not worth it.

The same suggestions go for performance-enhancing drugs. In the past, the deleterious effects of human growth hormone, blood doping, steroids, and so forth have ruined the life or health of many an athlete in later years. Young people think they are invincible. The truth is, they are not. For more information on these topics, read the excellent book by Dr. Steven Ungerleider, *Faust's Gold: Inside the East German Doping Machine* (2001). This book offers a chilling look at the incredible negative side effects and later results of illegal drugs used for peak performance in the East German regime. In their later years, many East German athletes developed serious health problems such as cancer. The illegal performance-enhancing drugs currently used will have many of the same physical results in the human body in later life. People just don't know what those results are yet.

So, take care of your body and feed it good nutritional food, get enough sleep (at least eight hours), rest, relax, and reduce physical and mental stress. If you do, your body will give you its best. All these things are important to give you a complete and well-rounded peak performance program.

Chapter 8

Troubleshooting Performance Blocks

Feel the fear and do it anyway.
Susan Jeffers

There is a law in psychology, the Yerkes-Dodson Law, that states in essence that if a little bit is good, a whole lot is not necessarily better. In other words, some anxiety, excitement, arousal, or anticipation is great for motivation, but too much decreases optimum performance. As an athlete, you must learn how to govern your emotions so that they work for you and not against you. What goes on in your mind before a competition? Are you afraid, excited, reluctant, or anxious? How you handle these thoughts and feelings is important to your peak performance.

Performance blocks range all the way from fear to illness. As an athlete, you must learn how to eliminate these blocks from your performance. The following are some of the more common problems or blocks in competition that you might encounter during your athletic career:

Negative self-talk

Choking, panicking, or freezing

Fear and anger

Physical illness, such as vomiting

Physical fatigue

Fear of failure, losing face, or looking bad or stupid

Hurting another athlete

Pressure from others, such as coaches, peers, or parents

Psyching out yourself instead of an opponent

Nervousness or anxiety

Negatively Speaking

Most of the blocks athletes experience come from negative self-talk and negative belief systems about themselves. Thoughts such as, *I don't have enough talent, I'm not good enough*, and *I am not disciplined enough*, all stand in the way of improvement. *I'm too young, I'm too old, I'm too tall, I'm too short*, and so forth are all limiting beliefs that keep athletes from achieving. These beliefs also help create the mind-set that makes athletes fearful in competitive situations.

Affirmations, when done consistently, help reframe or reprogram negative thought patterns. When you become conscious of what you are telling yourself in competition, you will begin to get a handle on how to get beyond the limitations of your mind. Every time you notice yourself saying negative things, acknowledge that you are doing it, be patient with yourself, and say something like, "Oh, there you go again; okay, let's get back to the positive." Then begin saying some of your affirmations to yourself: "I am as good as anyone here." "I enjoy competing." "I am strong and confident." "I am relaxed, alert, and ready to do my best." Or you can say single words or phrases such as, "positive," "I'm good," "strong and confident," "relaxed and alert," and so forth. With practice, such statements will become reassuring and calming influences for your mental state during competition.

People spend too much time seeking approval from others, when the most important approval must come from themselves. The comparison process enables people to continue an unhealthy cycle of approval seeking. Yes, they want and need acknowledgment; yes, they want and need love; but they often fail to see that these must come from within first, so they are unable to appreciate and accept these things from their families, peers, and coaches.

The affirmations in table 8.1 address these issues. Go through the list and select three or four categories that are relevant to you. Then select five affirmations from each category that seem hard for you to believe about yourself. Write these affirmations on a piece of paper, put it on your nightstand, and read them in the morning before you get out of bed and at night before you go to sleep. These affirmations will help you change your attitudes about yourself and your abilities.

Affirmations will help you think of yourself in a more positive light. Human beings live in such judgment of themselves and each

Table 8.1

Psyching yourself up	Perseverance	Handling rejection	Reframing and letting go of losses	Advocating for self
I am ready! I am hot! I hang in there. I just do it! I am aggressive and well-respected.	I am persistant. What I have to say is important. It is easy for me to keep going. I am patient.	I belong here. It is easy for me to hear no. I ask for what I want easily. I let go of any upset when I hear no. I handle rejection easily and turn it into a learning experience. I learn from these experiences.	It is okay to make a mistake. I learn from setbacks. I let go with ease and grace. It is okay and I am okay. I am patient. I find it easy to let go of self-criticism. I nurture and take care of myself.	I am important. What I say, need, or want is important. I deserve _____. I am worthy of respect. I trust and respect myself. I am proud of myself and my accomplishments.

Asking for what you want	Feeling overwhelmed	Being stressed	Handling success	Fearing the unknown
I ask for what I want clearly. This is important to me. I would like… Hearing yes or no is okay. I am patient. It is easy for me to ask for what I want. I am straightforward in asking for what I want. I deserve to have what I want.	I am centered and relaxed. I am strong, powerful, and centered. I listen easily. I am peaceful and harmonious in the midst of chaos. I work on an even pace emotionally. I deserve rest and relaxation.	My top priority is making sure I take an hour or a day to relax. I breathe fully and deeply. I am important to me. I see and use stressful situations as a challenge. I am patient and relaxed. I do one thing at a time, with care.	I take time to enjoy my successes. I acknowledge my successes (list them so you can remember them). This is fun! I nurture myself when I am busy. I deserve to succeed. I acknowledge and appreciate myself.	I welcome abundance and prosperity into my life. I acknowledge my successes. I am creating a successful reputation for myself. I am creating a successful and prosperous athletic career. I let in the praise of others.

other. This culture is based on comparison, and although analysis and comparison can be invaluable to people when applied to themselves and their accomplishments, comparison with others can create a lot of misery in their lives. This is because they often choose to come up short. If you must compare, do it in a positive way. Positive comparison heals; negative comparison hurts.

Before you break the cycle of comparison, you can change how you use it by comparing yourself to others and seeing your value, your uniqueness, and your positives, rather than your negatives. A soccer player I was working with used to torment herself by comparing herself with her teammates, always seeing her weaknesses and how she never quite measured up to them. Rather than trying to break her habit of comparing, I had her compare her strengths with her teammates'. Eventually, by acknowledging the comparison process and substituting affirmations for the negative comparisons, she was able to stop comparing herself to others.

Facing Your Fears

Fear can be a unique underlying motivator or destroyer in people's lives. Their fear often stops them from achieving what they desire, and it creates self-doubt and confusion in their minds. Many people become paralyzed, terrified, immobile, and sick with dread when they are fearful. Fear can turn people into victims, causing them to feel overwhelmed, weak, and helpless. They may feel empty, debilitated, and lost. And what are they afraid of? They're afraid of losing face, looking stupid, or looking like a failure to others. They are often afraid of themselves—their own power, success, and failure. Some people are afraid of love, hate, rejection, life and death, or simply the unknown.

When athletes are concerned with these fears, they are focusing outside themselves. Refocusing on their technique, their body, and their event, instead of on the crowd watching them, brings them back to the present moment and makes them internally focused. The successful athlete learns to ignore the crowd or uses its sounds as motivation to do better by thinking, *They are for me,* or *They want me to do well.* Even reframing a negative crowd is possible. Thinking, *I'll show them*, becomes a constructive tool. The old attitude of entering a competition motivated by challenge is quite acceptable in this case. The quiet inner knowing and

I trust my body and myself.

confidence of athletes sustains them even when the crowd is boo-ing. It is this inner reserve and confidence that brings forth peak performances. This state can be reached by using the centering and breathing technique, saying affirmations, and being relaxed, alert, and ready for competition. Successful athletes know not to take the crowd's emotional displays personally. These athletes remain within themselves and their performance.

I attended a workshop where the participants discussed what success meant to them and common fears about success. Many people enjoy sharing their successes with their friends and fam-ily. When they are afraid or doubt themselves, they look to their friends and family for support and encouragement. These people allow themselves to be vulnerable with their family members, be-ing open with all their feelings, both positive and negative. They trust that they will be loved for who they are, not for what they achieve or don't achieve. Sharing joys and sorrows with friends and family can help people feel proud, fulfilled, and supported.

To see how you look at success, take a few minutes now to write down quick answers to the questions on the How I Look at Suc-cess worksheet on page 128.

The answers from those who attended the workshop included receiving acknowledgment from others; a feeling of self-satisfaction, excitement, and energy; having enough money to live the lifestyle I enjoy; and being able to do work that I love doing. In looking at your answers, what things represent success to you? Is acknowledgment important? Is it self-satisfaction, what other people say to you, the excitement of winning, the energy you feel, the money you make? You must know what is important to you to achieve success and reach your goals.

And what do you say to yourself? Do you acknowledge your successes, or do you continue to raise the bar on yourself? Is your win ever good enough? Do you pat yourself on the back after a win? Or are you self-critical and judgmental?

Many athletes have powerful negative belief systems that keep them from success and prevent them from achieving their dreams. To counteract negative belief systems, athletes must identify these beliefs so that they can begin to reframe the negative thinking that surrounds them. Use the Identifying My Fears of Success worksheet on page 129 to identify your own fears of success in order to become more conscious of your own emotional process around being successful.

Visualization for Dealing With Fear

Find a comfortable place to sit or lie . . . begin to breathe deeply . . . taking a deep breath, holding it . . . and letting it go with a sigh . . . breathing in . . . and letting it out . . . breathing in energy . . . breathing out peace . . . relax your shoulders . . . your neck . . . soften your abdomen and belly . . . and begin to feel yourself to be centered, whole, and balanced . . . begin to imagine gold light coming into the top of your head, and down into your body, coming out through your solar plexus, just below your navel . . . feel your solar plexus to be powerful and strong . . . with the light and energy flowing out of it . . . feeling and seeing the light from the top of your head . . . flowing through your body and out through your solar plexus . . . feeling relaxed . . . powerful . . . and with a flexibility and suppleness around your solar plexus . . . imagine it pulsating with the passage of this energy from the top of your head and through it . . .

Begin to acknowledge your feelings of fear . . . remembering the list that you made . . . or a situation or risk that causes you to feel fearful . . . and as each fear comes up . . . acknowledge it and thank it for making itself known to you . . . take some time to think of each fear . . . acknowledge it and say to it, "I thank you, and I welcome you (and think of the fear), and I let you flow through me." Let yourself imagine the fear flowing through your solar plexus and flowing out through the middle of your back . . . just passing through as if you were transparent . . . the fear flows in and the fear flows out . . . there is no place for it to stay in your body . . . it is just flowing through you . . . moving on through your solar plexus as a light breeze . . . feel your solar plexus to be strong and flexible . . . letting the fear pass through it, without pain or anxiety, just as if you were watching or feeling a soft breeze . . . continue to imagine the light flowing down from the top of your head out through your solar plexus . . . feeling strong, powerful, and centered . . .

Begin to say your affirmations about your fears . . . "I belong here . . . it is okay to make a mistake . . . I learn from my mistakes . . . I let go with ease and grace . . . it is okay and I am okay . . . it is easy for me to let go of self-criticism . . . I nurture and take care of myself . . . I am proud of myself and my accomplishments . . . I trust myself and my abilities . . . I am strong and powerful . . . I am able to let go of my fears easily . . . I just do it!"

Begin to imagine yourself handling the situations you fear in a calm, comfortable, and powerful way . . . see, hear, and feel yourself succeeding . . . handling your anxiety . . . feeling powerful and in control . . . feeling your solar plexus to be strong and flexible . . . knowing you are good enough and are worthy of your accomplishments . . . feeling your strength and power . . . acknowledging your fear and letting it go . . . going on to succeed . . . to achieve your goals and dreams . . . knowing that you have what it takes to be successful and to overcome any obstacles, including any fear you might have or feel . . . you are good enough . . . you are worthy of respect and achievement . . .

Slowly let the images and feelings fade, remembering that you have everything within you to be, do, or have what you want in life . . . knowing you are enough and you deserve the best . . .

On a count of three, you can open your eyes . . . feeling strong, powerful, and confident . . . one . . . take a deep breath . . . letting it out . . . two . . . stretch your neck and shoulders . . . three . . . open your eyes when you're ready . . . feeling grounded, connected, and in your body.

How I Look at Success

How do you know when you are succeeding?

   a. How does succeeding feel to you? (Be specific.)

   b. What do you say to yourself and others when you are succeeding or when you feel successful?

   c. What do you look like when you are succeeding? What do you look like when you are successful?

When you are successful, what information do you receive from family, friends, peers, and the universe at large?

Identifying My Fears of Success

My own fears of success are:

1.

2.

3.

4.

Four affirmations to counter my fears:
(For example, if your fear was, "I'm afraid that if I'm as successful as I can be, I'll end up alone," two affirmations might be, "My success draws wonderful, loving people into my life," and "I enjoy my success with my partner and my friends.")

1.

2.

3.

4.

Taking Risks

Risk is the ability to take chances. In the dictionary, the word *risk* is defined as "exposing to danger." No wonder it is so hard for some people to risk! Leaders and peak performers see risk as taking a chance and trying something new and different. It's a little-mentioned fact that, in the same year that Babe Ruth hit the most home runs of his career, he also had the most strikeouts! He was willing to risk failure, losing face, and so on in order to achieve a record that stood for decades.

As discussed in chapter 1, in order to achieve, you must learn to risk and to do new things. If you want to create success in your life, and deal with your fear, it helps to go toward the fear instead of avoiding it. Please understand, this is not advocating that you do dangerous or unsafe activities. Fear is a healthy emotion when it comes to physical danger. The fears discussed here are fears generated by your feelings and emotions, not by physical danger. And with these emotional fears, it is helpful to acknowledge them and to decide to do something about them.

Try this exercise to see how you think and feel about the word *risk*. Take a couple of minutes and close your eyes, quieting your mind and breathing deeply. Look at the Risk worksheet, and begin quickly and without much thought to write whatever pops into your mind about risk.

Keep writing until you know you are finished, or for about five minutes. What have you written? These words will give you an idea of your own belief systems about risking or taking chances. It is completely normal to find that you've written things like "It's okay to let go," "I ask for what I want," "Breathe deeply," "Reach," "Heart pounding," or "Afraid to be vulnerable and open."

In her book, *Feel the Fear and Do It Anyway* (1988), Susan Jeffers says, "Pushing through the fear is less frightening than living with the underlying fear that comes from a feeling of help-lessness." In other words, the terror and anxiety that come from avoidance is much worse than the action you can take in doing something different. Making a short list of all the things that you are afraid of in a competitive situation helps you acknowledge and recognize your fears.

In dealing constructively with your fears, remember to use this process:

1. Acknowledge the fear, the setback, or the emotional feel-ings.
2. Breathe—deep breathing three to five breaths, from the top of your head down through your solar plexus.
3. Relax your shoulders, neck, and abdomen.
4. Say or write affirmations to counteract the fear.
5. Visualize dealing with your fear from a place of power and control.

There is acceptance and success in just being out there. By let-ting yourself be seen, by taking risks to do something different, you grow. Avoidance just doesn't work, and it makes you miserable by turning you into a victim. Sometimes the process of taking risks is as important as the outcome. Often it is what you learn by trying something new rather than what you achieve that matters.

Preventing Choking

Perhaps the most stinging criticism that can be directed toward athletes is that they choke. The comment implies an emotional

weakness under the pressure of competition that is the antithesis of what athletes want to portray to themselves, opponents, and fans.

Yet, all athletes have choked. And even though they will occasionally admit to a case of the nerves, they might not realize that there are other things going on that involve far more than the nervous system. There are steps they can take to deal with the problem.

In "Maintaining Technique Under Pressure" (2002), sport psychologist Jim Loehr, EdD, and former U.S. Davis Cup captain Tom Gullikson, have identified physical, emotional, and mental competencies. The competencies are arranged in a hierarchy that supports mechanical precision under pressure—in other words, preventing choking. The authors apply their model to tennis, but the principles can be implemented in almost any sport. Not surprisingly, the competencies they outline also involve supportive habits, all of which can be learned, developed, and refined to perform well and to avoiding choking.

In summary, Loehr and Gullikson have taken the tools of sport psychology and organized them into a framework that athletes can see, understand, and apply to their individual situations. Each mental and emotional habit except time management is addressed in this book. (You can find many excellent books about time management in your favorite bookstore.) For each of the three competencies, table 8.2 lists the habits required to support the competency, and the times during training and competition when the competency is most important. You can apply these competencies and habits to your own sport.

When athletes choke, it is usually because they are fearful or angry. Tennis players, for example, may begin choking and missing every shot, and then become more and more upset with themselves. When this happens, players lose the present focus—that of staying in the present moment—and continue to obsess about the blown shots and mistakes made in the past. Combined with negative thinking, this process interferes with concentration, focus, and confidence. To counter this type of block, you must calm yourself, center inside, and shift concentration to the present moment, focusing all mental attention on the upcoming shot. Letting go of the past, forgiving yourself for making errors, and refocusing on the present moment are crucial for getting beyond the mistakes and no longer expending mental energy on the missed shots. This may take considerable willpower. But the

Table 8.2   Habits That Enhance Peak Performance

Competencies	Supportive habits	When to implement them
Mental	Concentration	During and between matches
	Points	
	Goal setting	
	Visualization	
	Mental preparation	
	Time management	
	Self-talk	
Emotional	Self-awareness	During breaks in the action
	Self-control	
	Mistake management	
	Breath control	
	Body language	
Physical	Sound biomechanics	Between matches
	Efficient movement	
	Flexibility	
	Nutrition and hydration	
	Fitness	

Adapted, by permission, from Jim Brown, 2002, *Georgia Tech Sports Medicine & Performance Newsletter* 10 (6):2.

habit of doing this consciously begins to overcome the old habits of negative thinking and self-blame, enabling you to remain focused on the present moment of competition.

When choking comes from fear, you can use the same method. If you are scared, acknowledge the fear, saying to yourself, "Oh yes, here you are again, and I know you feel scared." Once you have acknowledged this fear, imagine the fear as a shrinking ball until it is a small, manageable size, or breathe deeply through your solar plexus. Instead of fighting or resisting the fear, acknowledge it and let it go. This way you decrease your own resistance to it, and it will not get in your way. You control it instead of it controlling you.

Fear before a competition can be dealt with in a variety of ways. You can use the positive and present focus techniques and the centering or relaxation techniques. You may also try remembering a successful and pleasant experience, either in practice or competition, where you were in complete control and performing confidently and well. It may help to imagine a very successful practice you had so that you see, hear, and feel all the bodily sensations you had when performing competently and successfully. All these feelings and sensations of competency and control will bring your body to a different physical state, replacing the fear with confidence and calmness. The reconnection with positive energy will reframe your current experience. You are recalling the confidence and well-being you felt in practice. This transfer of skills from practice to competition is an important tool for you to remember. You can, at any time, recall and summon the strength, power, and accuracy you felt during a good practice or previous competition. The visualizations in this chapter will give you more specific ideas on how to do this.

For runners with prerace fears, it helps to do progressive relaxation and a mental rehearsal or visualization of the course every day for at least a week before a big race. By doing so, you will have control over the fear, and you can replace it with feelings of strength, relaxation, and familiarity. Say your affirmations to yourself, and see yourself on the course, running strong and well within yourself. Do this in your mind's eye as discussed in previous chapters. Other runners prefer to use prerecorded, guided visualization running tapes of specific races because they can focus their entire attention on the voices or words. Not having to exercise the mental discipline to do it within themselves, they relax and let the tape do the work for them. Their minds wander less often with this method, and the tapes help create a sense of peace, well-being, and anticipation.

People use the 5K, 10K, or marathon race visualizations for other reasons too. It was surprising to learn that one man, a writer, listened to the marathon tape and was so energized by it that he sat down and wrote for three hours as fast as he could, turning out one of his best pieces of work. He said he felt exhilarated and full of energy. A woman runner listened to the tape as she awoke one morning. She then got up and had the most beautiful run she had had in months, noticing all the trees, grass, dew, and flowers. Athletes are so often unaware of their environment as they pass it by. Listening to tapes that describe sights, sounds, and internal feelings can stimulate your awareness of your surroundings and make you take notice. You may want to write your own script for a visualization, and record it for yourself.

Breathing Through a Block

"Breathe!" "What? Of course I breathe." Notice that when you are tense, uptight, fearful, or nervous, you begin to hold your breath. This is a natural response when someone is not relaxed. As the tensions of the day increase, people tend to breathe more shallowly. One of the cornerstones of a state of relaxation is good, deep breathing. I often tease the athletes I work with by spontaneously asking, "Are you breathing?" And it is true—many times they are not breathing regularly. It will help you to begin noticing in any tense situation, either athletic or in your personal or work life, whether or not you are holding your breath or breathing shallowly. If you are, make an effort to breathe deeply and fully to create a more relaxed state of mind and physical well-being.

If you panic or freeze, you should concentrate on breathing deeply and do a short centering and focusing sequence while sitting, standing, or lying down. Close your eyes for a moment, bring your attention inward, and again call for the feelings of confidence and control from previous practices or events. Physical movement may help get rid of excess energy as well. Physical movement changes mental states, so activities such as stretching, jogging briefly or in place, or simply walking while being aware of your breathing should help you control feelings of panic. Paying attention to your breathing is most important. Concentrate on maintaining relaxed, full breaths.

Wallowing in the fear accomplishes nothing. You must acknowledge and control your fear, then take positive actions to begin thinking differently. Affirmations may help return you to a more controlled and peaceful state of mind. You may also want to explore visualizations, such as the following, to help you bring feelings of confidence and competence to any competitive situation.

Visualization for Confidence

Feel yourself to be centered, at peace, and relaxed. With your mind's eye, begin to see yourself at a workout where you were performing at your absolute best . . . where you were performing perfectly and you felt competent and confident . . . a time when you absolutely knew that you knew and you were in complete control of your body and mind . . . a time when you knew completely that you were right on . . . a workout where you were at your peak physically and mentally . . . you were in control and having fun . . . there was no pressure and it was easy. See yourself at that workout right now. Notice what you are wearing and how the people around you look. Become aware of how it felt deep inside of you when you knew you were absolutely right on . . . competent . . . in control . . . perfect. Take a look at those feelings . . . you felt comfortable and relaxed . . . after all, it was just a workout . . . you were loose. What were you saying to yourself?

As you become aware of those feelings, choose a word or a short phrase that reminds you of those feelings . . . a word that makes you think of those feelings . . . makes you feel those feelings again. Picture the word in your mind . . . say it over to yourself . . . remember the feelings. And then think of your perfect performance . . . the way you looked . . . what you heard . . . how you felt. Feel the experience deeply and say the word over to yourself. Notice how the word brings back that experience of fun and ease and makes you feel and see yourself at your peak . . . performing perfectly. Say the word over to yourself and allow yourself to feel those feelings of being absolutely perfect.

Now . . . think of your goal in your next big competition and begin to see yourself there . . . at your next competition. The goal you have in mind is very important. Say this goal over in your mind. When you have the goal well in mind, begin to see yourself achieving this goal and remember the relaxed, easy feelings you had at that great workout. Start at the beginning of the competition . . . watch . . . listen . . . feel and smell everything you can as you move closer and closer to achieving this goal. It is as easy as a workout . . . no pressure, no tightness . . . you are smooth and in control . . . relaxed and having fun. Remember your affirmations now . . . say them over to yourself . . . say those phrases that support your goal . . . say your word . . . watch yourself coming closer and closer to your goal, feeling comfortable, having fun . . . you are light and smooth and loose. Notice how it feels inside . . . what you are saying to yourself . . . feel it in your heart . . . remember the special word you just gave yourself and how it connects you with all those feelings of competence . . . confidence and well-being, relaxation, ease, and strength . . . allow yourself to stay in those feelings as you see yourself finally reaching your goal . . . competing at your highest level . . . feeling good . . . having fun. Become aware of what happens now that you have succeeded. What is happening around you? What is happening within you? Are people congratulating you . . . are you alone? Feel the peaceful inner knowledge that you have done what you set out to do . . . you have done it well . . . it feels just as easy to compete as it feels at a good workout. Allow yourself to experience all of those feelings and the knowledge and success . . .

Know that any time you want to call up those feelings again . . . any time you want to have that sense of competency, ease, relaxation, and enjoyment, all you have to do is center yourself, take a deep breath, and say your special word or phrase to yourself to reconnect with those feelings . . . now begin to watch the scene of your successful competition float away from you . . . watch it becoming dimmer . . . let it go . . . you remember how it feels . . . know that you are perfectly capable of achieving it any time you choose as you begin to come back into the peace in your mind . . . the relaxation in your body . . . the quiet of the room . . . come back to your breathing . . . notice how steady it is . . . breathe deeply into your belly . . . filling your chest with air . . . hold it . . . and let it go. On a count of three you may come back into the room . . . one . . . you begin to move a little and reconnect with your body . . . two . . . move your arms and legs . . . three . . . you may open your eyes when you are ready.

Managing Anger

Reflect for a moment on how anger makes you feel . . . feel the anger in your body . . . where do you feel it? Is it in your heart . . . your chest . . . your mind . . . feel the heat of the anger in your chest . . . constricting, tightening your chest and body . . . feel the pain that anger brings to your body and mind . . .

Such were the words I heard at a 1977 retreat. They were spoken by Stephen Levine, the author of *Guided Meditations, Explorations and Healings* (1991). Before then, I hadn't thought much about anger. These words were the first part of a guided meditation on forgiveness and letting go of anger. I was struck by the power of this meditation and by how bad my body felt when I imagined feeling anger.

Over the past 10 years, anger has become a major issue in athletic competition. Sport psychologists have spent many hours counseling players on how to control their tempers. The psychologists work with the athletes to help them express their anger in settings other than athletic competition. Think back to the steps you must take in acknowledging fear. These same steps can be applied to controlling and managing anger.

Again, here they are:

1. Acknowledge your anger and feelings.
2. Breathe to calm yourself—three to five deep breaths, from the top of your head down to your solar plexus and out.
3. Relax your shoulders, neck, and abdomen.
4. Say and write affirmations for controlling anger.
5. Visualize feeling relaxed and in control.

Later, go home or somewhere safe and get the anger out of your body, perhaps by beating a pillow, chopping wood, screaming in your car with the windows up, writing all of your feelings on paper and burning it—whatever you need to do to let the feelings go and to get them out of your body.

Anger is a natural process, one to be expressed and observed. A small amount of anger can be very motivating and can be a powerful force in athletic achievement. The problem with using anger as a motivator is that most people have great difficulty controlling it. When people are really angry, anger controls them, and they often give up their personal power and integrity when they "lose it." Anger must be expressed and released from your body. Unexpressed anger can turn into illness or uncontrollable rage, enslaving your body and mind.

Many professional players are in control even when they are angry. They seem to use anger as a vent for aggression and to distract their opponents. Unfortunately, younger players use the professionals as role models for anger, but the younger players are not in control of themselves on the court. Their fury serves no better purpose than to blow their concentration, and it wins them penalties rather than points.

On the other hand, many people are what are referred to as conflict avoiders. Conflict avoiders put up massive resistance to anger, avoiding conflict at all costs. They become placaters and are terrified of confrontation. Many see anger as being out of control of their emotions, which is unacceptable to them. These people may believe anger is bad, and they may feel a lot of shame or guilt about anger and its expression. They may also think that any emotions that look out of control, such as crying or being angry, are totally unacceptable. Such belief systems often result in people disassociating from their emotions and true feelings, and eventually may lead to illness.

I am calm, cool, and collected under pressure.

© SportsChrome

People who overexpress anger may be doing so to manipulate their environment to create safety or protection for themselves. Some people may try to make others angry to make those others feel guilty. In any case, every time you get angry with someone, you give up your personal power and integrity.

Anger can be expressed without dumping all over the person you are angry with. Often anger is a result of feelings of resentment that you may harbor for friends or opponents. Resentment is often the killer of friendships and relationships, especially when anger is unexpressed and ignored. Resentment binds you, keeps you down, creates feelings of powerlessness, and holds you back from your achievements. Feelings of resentment can make you want to withdraw, withhold information, blame others, feel trapped, and become a victim. Part of you shrinks inside, your heart closes, and you feel hurt and pain.

Take a couple of minutes to write down what thoughts and words come to mind about the word *anger*. Write your words on the Anger worksheet.

In doing this exercise, you will uncover some of your belief systems about anger. You may come up with words such as "overwhelming," "out of control," "motivation," or "concentrated." These words represent a number of feelings you may have about anger and your expression of it. Remember, you are not these feelings; these are simply things you do and feel.

For example, two players had major issues concerning anger on the court. Both were young men; one played tennis and one played basketball. They were both 16. After three sessions each, both had good control of their tempers during games and tournaments.

The basketball player, Eric, found success by focusing on his strengths, saying and remembering affirmations about those strengths. He also used a few affirmations about letting go of anger and missed shots. The following affirmations were helpful to Eric:

I'm a smart player.

I'm the best defensive player on the team.

I'm aggressive.

I'm a good team player.

I've got a good positive attitude.

I'm quick and fast.

I mentally let go of missed shots easily.

I play more aggressively each game, especially on offense.

I am as relaxed in games as I am in practice.

I am calm, cool, and collected on the court.

I easily forgive myself for missed shots.

I have good concentration and focus in the game.

I stop worrying about what people think.

I let go of what people think about me.

I have fun playing.

The tennis player, Shane, would get furious with himself if he started to lose or miss shots. His negative self-talk included cursing at himself, saying to himself, "Dummy, hit the ball right! You're playing like #%@*. You can't lose to this joke." If he got mad, he would stay mad and end up blowing the match. Here are the affirmations that helped Shane:

I forgive myself for missing a point.

I encourage and support myself with my talk.

I let go of mistakes and focus on the next shot.

Between points, I let go of the last point and think about the next shot.

I play aggressively and well, especially if I'm behind.

I think positively during a match.

I am mentally tough in each match I play.

When I'm ahead, I play even more aggressively.

I love playing well, and I have fun playing.

I am calm, cool, and collected on the court.

I have a positive attitude.

I am a cool dude.

Use the Personal Anger Awareness worksheet to think about what things make you angry and how you can deal with that anger.

Personal Anger Awareness

Take a minute or two to think about what things make you angry when you are playing or competing.

1. I get angry when:

    a.

    b.

    c.

    d.

2. How I am currently dealing with my anger during competition:

    a.

    b.

    c.

    d.

3. How I would like to constructively handle my anger in competition:

    a.

    b.

    c.

    d.

4. Five affirmations to help me handle my anger in a positive way:

    a.

    b.

    c.

    d.

    e.

The following visualization may be helpful to you in reframing and releasing any anger you experience in competition. As with all visualizations, select one of the relaxation sequences in chapter 5 to quiet your mind and body before the visualization process.

Visualization for Dealing With Anger

Find a comfortable place to sit or lie . . . begin to breathe deeply . . . taking a deep breath, holding it . . . and letting it go with a sigh . . . breathing in . . . and letting it out . . . breathing in energy . . . breathing out peace . . . relax your shoulders . . . your neck . . . soften your abdomen and belly . . . and begin to feel yourself to be grounded, whole, and balanced . . . begin to imagine gold light coming into the top of your head from above, and down into your body, coming out through your solar plexus . . . feel your solar plexus to be powerful and strong . . . with the light and energy flowing out of it . . . feeling and seeing the light from the top of your head . . . flowing through your body and out through your solar plexus . . . feeling relaxed . . . powerful . . . and with a flexibility and suppleness around your solar plexus . . . imagine it pulsating with the passage of this energy from the top of your head and through it . . .

Think of the last time you were angry in a competition or practice . . . or of the list you just made on anger . . . begin to acknowledge any feelings of anger you might have during competition or practice . . . remembering the list of things that make you angry . . . and as each item of anger comes up . . . acknowledge it and thank it for making itself known to you . . . take some time to think of each angry thought . . . acknowledge it and say to it, "I thank you, and I welcome you (and think of being angry); my anger is welcome here; you are welcome here and I acknowledge you and let you flow through me." Let yourself imagine the angry feelings flowing through your solar plexus and flowing out through the middle of your back . . . just passing through, as if you were transparent . . . the anger flows in and the anger flows out . . . there is no place for it to stay in your body . . . it is just flowing through you . . . imagine yourself surrendering to the flow . . . the anger moving on through your solar plexus as a light breeze . . . and feel your belly and abdomen to be strong and flexible . . . letting the angry feelings pass through the area above your waist, without pain or anxiety, just as if you were watching or feeling a soft breeze . . . continue to imagine the light flowing down from the top of your head out through your solar plexus . . . feeling strong, powerful, and centered . . .

Begin to say your affirmations about your anger . . . "I let go of my anger easily . . . I am in control of myself on the court . . . I am powerful and centered . . . it is easy for me to forgive myself . . . I easily let go of mistakes or missed shots . . . I am calm, cool, and collected . . . I am mentally tough . . . I am focused and concentrated . . . I encourage and support myself . . . I am a positive player." Begin to imagine yourself handling your anger in a calm, comfortable, and powerful way . . . see, hear, and feel yourself succeeding . . . handling your anger . . . feeling powerful and in control . . . feeling your solar plexus to be strong and flexible . . . knowing you are in control and are worthy of your accomplishments . . . feeling your strength and power . . . acknowledging your anger and letting it go . . . going on to succeed . . . to achieve your goals and dreams . . . knowing that you have what it takes to be successful and to overcome any obstacles, including any anger you might feel . . . you *are* good enough . . . you *are* worthy of respect and achievement . . . you *are* safe and in control . . . you *are* powerful . . . begin to remember a time when you were totally confident and in control of yourself during a competition or in practice . . . allow yourself to see, feel, and hear the events of that time . . . let all the images come back to your awareness . . . feeling the feelings of pride, joy, freedom . . . all the power and strength of that time . . . your own self-approval . . . self-acceptance . . . that feeling of well-being and a job well done . . . the feelings of competence and confidence . . . perhaps of you helping your teammates, or them helping you . . . working together as a team . . . allow yourself to experience that time again . . . seeing, hearing, and feeling the events . . . and think of a word that represents those thoughts and feelings . . . saying the word over to yourself . . . knowing that word will bring back all of those feelings of confidence and control . . . and remember that you can say that word to yourself any time you feel angry, and the anger will dissipate easily, and you will experience feelings of confidence, power, and control . . . easily dropping any anger you might feel . . . becoming confident and powerful, focused and in control . . . remember your word . . . the word that transforms anger into confidence and control . . . knowing that you can say your word any time you wish to remember these positive feelings (pause); slowly begin to let the images and feelings fade, remembering that you have everything within you to be, do, or have what you want in life . . . knowing you can acknowledge and control your anger any time you wish . . . knowing that you are worthy of the best . . . remembering your word . . .

On a count of three, you can open your eyes . . . feeling strong, powerful, and confident . . . one . . . take a deep breath . . . letting it out . . . two . . . stretch your neck and shoulders . . . three . . . open your eyes when you're ready . . .

Fear and anger are two strong and powerful emotions. If you open up to these feelings and are comfortable in acknowledging and expressing them, you can overcome most mental obstacles in your journey toward success. What you move toward and through, you overcome; what you resist, you may intensify, exaggerate, or become.

Feeling External Pressures

Often a mental block develops because of a poor relationship between a coach and an athlete or team. Coaches must learn to handle athletes with different temperaments in different ways. A hard-line, aggressive approach may work well with one athlete and not with another. Some athletes need support and positive feedback rather than criticism and negative feedback. Often this negative approach fails, and some coaches are not willing to be "softer" with certain players. But athletes have control over how they handle what the coach is giving out.

For example, a high school player was constantly upset because the coach was "riding" him. After a number of relaxation sessions, along with guided visualizations of himself playing well—which included hearing the coach's jibes and seeing the comments roll off him—he started to play better. Learning that he, the athlete, had control over how he took the coach's comments gave him some freedom, and he learned to ignore the negativity of the coach. Many coaches, while seeing themselves as realistic, subtly undermine their players' confidence by making negative comments to the press. Simple statements such as, "I was surprised we won," or "I'm not sure we're ready . . . we'll just go out and see what we'll do," are meant to be conservative and realistic. These statements are often seen as negative by the athletes, who may

A coach's strategy and positive feedback help build athletes' confidence and improve performance.

feel fit and ready to go. After such comments, the athletes begin to feel a lack of support and often question themselves and their confidence.

Athletes sometimes fool themselves into thinking they are better than they are and can't accept it when a coach doesn't let them play. These athletes become antagonistic toward the coach, blame him, and are generally disgruntled and unhappy. Once athletes accept the responsibility for playing or not playing, they tend to improve and be more satisfied with their position. Again, remember that you are in control of your feelings about the coach, the game, and other athletes. Feelings of antagonism and anger directed at the coach or another athlete may sometimes help motivate you, but usually these feelings interfere with peak performance and are counterproductive.

Speaking of coaches, choosing a coach or a club is important, and you should explore all the possibilities in your area. The personalities of coaches and athletes are sometimes compatible and sometimes not. Even if a coach has coached many world-class successful athletes, sometimes the fit isn't right. Here are some guidelines to think about when selecting a coach, a team, or a club.

- Choose carefully by getting expert opinions about a club or coach. Ask for references. Talk to other athletes who are being coached by the person. Ask for a list of a few athletes who are no longer being coached by the person or no longer belong to the club. Find out why these athletes changed coaches and what they think about the coaching they received. Relying on the coach's integrity is essential. It is also your right to get good information about the coach and the program from other athletes.

- The creation of good communication and trust between coaches and athletes is essential. Athletes must be able to trust their coaches and believe what their coaches tell them. Quietly collect as much information about the coach as you can, getting as much objective information as possible.

- Instill in yourself a feeling of self-trust. Know what is comfortable, uncomfortable, and right for you on all levels—physically, mentally, and emotionally.

- Any coach who uses corporal punishment or verbally abuses athletes should be avoided.

- Above all, trust your own intuition, and if you are not enjoying the coaching, the workouts, or the group, then look for someone else who is more compatible with your needs and personality.

Other problems in competition often stem from peer pressure or pressure from parents. Not playing, not succeeding, and "riding the bench" all tend to undermine confidence and create fear about performing at all. If you can concentrate on watching other players and turning the experience of bench sitting into learning, it will be to your benefit. This will keep you from psyching yourself out and putting yourself down. If you see yourself as a loser, you will create this atmosphere around you. If you are "unattached" to playing or not playing, you will feel better about yourself and won't be riding a roller coaster of emotions. Make a game out of watching the best players in great detail—their form, how they breathe, their temperament—all the nuances you can see, hear, or feel about their performance. Let those who are pressuring you know that you are learning from the best and that it is important to you. It is part of your training. Imitate what you like about those players' style and learn something new. In this case,

I find joy in the moment and a love for the game.

© SportsChrome

it benefits you to be outwardly focused. You can learn a lot from others while waiting for your turn to compete.

Supporting your team or fellow athletes with enthusiasm helps you stay "up." Many times, being supportive is as important as participating. Let go of your ego, focus on the moment, and support others as well as yourself, regardless of what your peers or parents expect of you.

Struggling With Illness

Some athletes are so fearful and upset before a major competition that they vomit. This condition may be difficult to control. Listening to relaxation tapes for a week or two before competition, and visualizing themselves as confident and in control of their mental process and physical state may help this condition. Athletes with this condition should also work with a sport psychologist to learn how to balance the nervousness and fear with physical and mental relaxation, calmness, and a sense of well-being. Spending time alone before the competition may be a help or a hindrance, depending on the athlete. Some athletes need the quiet time alone to prepare themselves mentally using a series of relaxation procedures. Gymnasts often sit alone and calm themselves, or actively practice their tricks alone in corners of the room, before they compete. For others, being with someone else or a group has a calming or diverting effect that helps them stay more in control of their precompetition jitters.

Athletes cope with the stress of competition in different ways. If a technique works for you, use it. If it is not working for you, be willing to try something new. Many times an athlete uses distraction just prior to competition. If this works, it's fine. Something else might work better, however. Be willing to try new ideas to discover what might help long-standing mental blocks in competition. Too often, athletes continue patterns and habits that don't work for them and fail to try new things that might make a difference in their performance. The key is to experiment until you find something that works even better for you. Be willing to risk and experiment with new techniques.

Fighting Back Fatigue

Physical fatigue can be overcome mentally. Alberto Salazar, a great marathon runner, ran himself almost to death's door in races, often suffering from internal dehydration. He was so mentally tenacious that he ran until he collapsed. He told himself that he might be hurting but the other guy was hurting too, so he ran harder. He wanted to win, and he was willing to go through pain to do so. Many elite athletes acknowledge their pain and use it. Focusing on their form, breathing, or other (pain-free) body parts enables them to handle the discomfort and fatigue rather than be disabled by it. It is all part of what is called "mental toughness."

Concentrating on your breathing patterns will help you deal with physical fatigue. It will divert your attention from your muscles. Full in-and-out breaths oxygenate the system and revive tired muscles. Visualizing white light or gold energy coming into the lungs often brings a feeling of lightness to the body and a surge of new energy, refreshing the athlete. Imagining moving your body, or legs and arms, as if strings are attached and someone else is giving them the energy often helps. It is best to concentrate on body or form to keep your concentration focused on yourself in general and not on the specific area that feels tired or painful. Disassociation, while giving some relief, allows you only to survive. It does not facilitate maximum performance. Total concentration and focus on the present event is what is needed during peak performance. You must continue to focus on the event, moment by moment by moment, being present in every moment.

Injuring Another Athlete

The fear of hurting another athlete is a common problem in contact sports. During your performance, if you can remember that you are not responsible for another person's experience, it will help you overcome this block. This chapter has talked about blame and letting go of blaming others for your experiences. You have a responsibility to play fairly and ethically. Most athletes in contact sports play with the understanding that they may be hurt or may inadvertently hurt another. You are all playing with the same risks and acceptance of these risks. If you are clearly outmatched or clearly superior, it may be difficult. However, you should play your best and want to win. You must let the other athletes assume responsibility for their experience and performance. Fear of hurting another will hold you back and will be an impediment to your performance.

Psyching Yourself Up

In psyching yourself up, you psych out your opponent. Marilyn King, an American pentathlete on the Olympic team, talked about how she entered the last event, the 800 meters, jumping around, looking full of energy and ready to go. Part of it was to psych herself up and to get her energy moving, and the other part was to intimidate her opponents who were also dog tired. One athlete said to her later, "I hated seeing you with so much energy when I was so tired. It was depressing. You always looked confident and ready."

You must create upbeat images of yourself and for yourself. Look, feel, and act confident. Look ready and calm and in complete control. "I am strong, powerful, and quick." "I am relaxed and confident." "I am full of energy and life." "I am as good or better than anyone at the starting line." All these affirmations create positive intent and consciousness. Power words such as *light, easy, fast, accurate, calm, relaxed, centered, strong,* and *powerful* help create a positive image and feeling within you. Affirmations can be important in shifting your focus from the negative frame of mind you may fall into when you push to your physical limits. Something as simple as "This is good for me" said during a hard workout when you feel fatigue can keep you going.

Overcoming Your Blocks

Obviously, when you overcome your performance blocks, you increase your chances of succeeding and reaching your peak performance. This chapter has given you some examples of the most common blocks and information on how to eliminate them. In summary, for success in overcoming blocks in competition, you must practice the following:

- Relaxing, centering, and focusing before and during competition.
- Transforming feelings of competence and ability from practice or past competitions to feelings of confidence in present competition.
- Visualizing yourself competing with control and confidence.
- Turning anger and disappointment into productiveness and positive feelings, not depression.
- Taking total responsibility for your behavior and not blaming others for your mistakes or losses.
- Letting others be responsible for their own experience.
- Using affirmations for self-support and confidence.

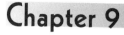

Chapter 9

Mental Training for Specific Needs

What you can do or dream you can—begin it. Boldness has genius, power and magic in it. Begin it now.
Goethe

In previous chapters, you have learned the tools you need to create a mental training program. Sometimes different circumstances require people to face different mental hurdles. Injured athletes have to deal with the physical and mental pain that accompanies their injury. Parents and youth coaches need to figure out the best approach for improving the mental skills of young athletes. Women athletes face belief systems that can hold them back from performing at their peak. This chapter addresses these issues and describes how to adapt mental training techniques to these specific circumstances.

Coping With an Injury

Perhaps you have learned this mental training program easily. Your physical body is improving, your mental "body" is improving, and then, *wham*, you're injured. Then what? Coping with injury is one of the most difficult parts of training. You see your teammates and competitors exercising, competing, practicing their techniques, and having fun while you sit on the sidelines. You feel yourself losing your stamina and strength, and you begin to believe you are losing your edge. All this can be depressing at best. What can you do to combat your feelings of helplessness and frustration? The mental training program described in this book can be applied to the healing process by developing the following:

- Injury-healing and pain control techniques
- An inner-guide process to help you heal yourself
- A mental training program for dealing with injury
- A visualization program for healing the injury

Coping With Pain and Injuries

One of the most difficult aspects of being an athlete is learning to cope with injuries. Injured athletes may feel themselves losing stamina and strength and may begin to believe they are losing their edge. Because of the importance of athletic performance to many athletes, an injury often leads to an attack on the self-image and loss of self-confidence. Injured athletes may feel sorry for themselves, they may exaggerate and believe that their career is ended, and they may decrease their motivation and increase their anxiety; all these reactions are extreme forms of negative self-talk. Basically, injured athletes feel that they have lost control of their bodies and, therefore, that they have lost control of their training, performance, and perhaps their future.

When you are injured, or in pain, you may become angry at yourself or your body parts. This anger makes it harder for you to heal. Resistance to pain creates more intensity in the pain because what you resist, you create, exaggerate, or become. The very act of resistance is a powerful creative force. Resistance is similar to negative self-talk because it creates negativity and a negative power. Bringing the pain or injury into your heart, literally letting go of the fear and anger connected with your pain or injury, helps you to work with it in a constructive manner. Such acceptance and acknowledgment creates an internal climate for healing injury and lessening pain. It is not giving up; it is merely deciding to stop fighting the pain or the injury. Send the pain or injury loving energy and acknowledge its importance to you as a learning experience. Look for its message and reason in your life. This is not easy, but it can be helpful to your self-awareness of body, mind, and spirit.

In ancient healing and spiritual traditions, the power of a positive mental attitude and the use of imagery were often major parts of the healing process. Researchers are now finding this tradition to be a valid one. Carl Simonton and Norman Cousins, both pioneers in holistic medicine, and other researchers in psychoneuroimmunology (PNI), have shown that the brain can send signals along nerves to enhance defenses against infection and pump out chemicals that make the body fight more aggressively. Though most of today's scientific research is being done on the recovery from major illness, scientists are finding the same techniques work with the healing of athletic injuries. These techniques stress the need for athletes to be involved in the control of their body's process toward health.

People are taught to run from their pain, especially the psychological pain. They are encouraged to tough it out, to be a man, to resist pain, to avoid the unpleasant physical and mental pain of life. But the key is opening your heart to your pain, injury, feelings, thoughts, and dreams. This means opening to the pain instead of resisting the pain. Stephen Levine, a therapist who works with the terminally ill, talks about opening your heart to yourself . . . to your pain and to your suffering (1987). When you open your heart to yourself, you can open your heart to others, treating them with respect and acceptance. In this life, pain may be inevitable, but suffering is optional.

If you want to recover, you must be tenacious in focusing on healing, and you must be hopeful about the outcome. You may want to get some counseling to learn to deal with social and emotional problems. Recovery means setting goals and finding reasons to take joy in every day. Most important, it means doing mental imagery exercises for healing your injury three times a day. A sport psychologist may begin by setting physical healing goals with you. For example, if you want to be performing pain free within the next three weeks, and to be strong and able to work out with a healthy body in that amount of time, then you should write down each of these goals as clearly and specifically as possible. (Time limits depend on the extent of the injury and the recommendation of a doctor, trainer, or coach.) For some injuries, it is necessary to write short-term and intermediate goals. These goals may have to do with flexibility or preliminary workouts such as physical movements in a pool or hot tub.

Once goals have been written, your attitude must be confronted: What are your fears and major frustrations? How do you view your body? What is your present level of motivation? Have you acknowledged that your body is injured or in pain? "Some view it as a disaster, others see it as an opportunity to display courage and still others welcome it as a relief from the drudgery of practice or the embarrassment and frustration of poor performance, lack of playing time or a losing season" (Rotella and Heyman 1993). Once your attitude has been assessed, you should form affirmations to assist you in establishing positive mental energy and to help you establish beliefs about personal control in the healing and strength of your body. Affirmations such as, "I am becoming stronger and healthier every day," "I am healing my body," "I am healing more and more every day," and "My body heals quickly and well," are typical and powerful. Because affirmations are used to counteract negative thoughts and energy that may prolong the healing process, they should be read at least once every day.

An important element of self-healing is a mental image that projects a positive future outcome. A visualization can stimulate your mind and body and create a positive intention for healing. As with all performance visualizations, you should begin healing imagery exercises with a deep relaxation process. In addition to the standard components of all visualizations (the use of all five senses and so forth), a visualization for healing should include the following elements:

- Acknowledgment of the injury.
- A dialogue between the athlete and the injured body part—asking the injury what it wants and making a commitment to give it what it wants.
- Forgiveness of the injured part and the body as a whole.
- Sending the injured part love and nurturing, sometimes in the form of a green, gold, or white light.
- Visualizing the injury healing and then whole and healthy.

You must also continue to visualize your technique in your sport while the body is healing. You should continue to attend practice and mentally rehearse each movement, every detail of performance, in order to keep your technique sharp and well ingrained while healing is taking place. This is also a way to support your teammates.

Implementing Your Own Program

In creating your own mental training program for injury, begin with the goal-setting exercise and create physical healing goals for yourself. Write these goals down using Mental Trainer #9. After writing your goals—two short-term, two intermediate, and two long-term—write affirmations for each goal, such as "I am performing pain free," "I am strong and healthy," and "I am healing more and more every day."

Now, pick the five affirmations that are the most important to you, write them on note cards, and put them around the house where you will see them often. Also, read them and say them to yourself at least twice a day, preferably in the morning and before bed at night. These messages will begin to counteract your negative thoughts about your injury. They will begin to change your focus from one of frustration that centers on the pain and problem to one of self-control, healing, and wholeness.

You will soon notice that your self-talk has become more and more positive. People often say negative things to themselves that they would not permit others to say to them. Positive images

Mental Trainer #9:   Self-Healing

Short-term goals for healing:

Affirmations:

Intermediate goals for healing:

Affirmations:

Long-term goals for healing:

Affirmations:

and self-affirming statements have tremendous positive mental power.

The third step in this healing program is, of course, the visualization process. For injury, begin with the relaxation process as usual, then continue to mentally visualize yourself practicing, improving your form and technique, and performing well, with strength and endurance. See yourself whole and with a healthy body. Imagine yourself performing exactly as you want to perform, without pain or weakness. To visualize your entire performance clearly, mentally practice your workout routine and competition. You should see yourself healthy and winning.

You may want to watch videotapes of yourself performing or watch technique videos of your sport, imagining yourself as the focal point. See yourself performing and succeeding, and instill yourself with desire. Make this a desire to recover, to be the best, to win. What you want athletically must be so compelling and powerful that nothing will stand in your way. This desire is such a powerful energy source that it will enable you to achieve anything you want to do.

Watch your teammates practice. Many athletes hate to watch when they are injured, but reframing your attitude while watching will help you learn to support fellow athletes. Pretend that you are the coach, or a camera, and watch each performer, analyzing his or her form, technique, strategy, and any weaknesses or strengths. This will help you later when you compete with them as well as help you focus on their present level of skills instead of on your frustrations.

As before, keep a mental training log, but this time for your injuries, tracking how you cope with "temporary retirement." For example, one athlete said that as she read back through her log, she noticed she had gone through all the stages of loss during her injury. The stages, outlined by Elisabeth Kubler-Ross (1997), are denial, anger, bargaining, depression, and acceptance. The movement through these stages is a healthy process as long as you do not stay stuck in one stage, such as anger or depression, too long. The athlete found that the mental log helped her move through these stages at a healthy pace, and soon she was well on her way to performing again.

A former University of Oregon athlete, who is also a former NCAA 800- and 1500-meter champion, is a great example of the power of positive thinking and visualization. After five surgeries in two years, she was not only running again, but she was racing without pain. She finished one second behind the winner in the national cross country championships, and she consistently raced faster with each passing month. She was a master of positive mental training. I asked her how she coped mentally with the injuries and surgery, and how she kept going in the face of all odds. Her story details common situations that occur with injured athletes:

It wrecked my Olympic hopes for that year. After my coach and I talked a while, I just started focusing on other goals . . . the world championships, other meets, and world records. I looked ahead. He told me, "You're 22. You have years ahead of you. Look at the long term. Get healthy now. Just get healthy." He helped me a lot. A lot of people who I thought were my friends just faded away. Initially, that really upset me. It was hard for people to talk to me because conversation focused around running, so it was awkward. It was hard after running so well and being so successful not to be able to do it. I wanted to do it so badly. I really struggled with anger. I hated hearing people complain about training. I wanted to run and couldn't and they were complaining. This was just a stage I went through. I realized that in the long run I'll be a stronger person after going through all this. I really proved to myself that I don't give up. I wasn't able to do the running part but I didn't lose anything physically. I lifted weights and biked and swam. My fitness remained at a real high level.

In terms of mental training, I have always used the mental techniques the team was taught. I imagine the injury getting better, I counsel myself, I get myself to stop worrying. We did formal relaxation sessions in high school; I use it unconsciously now. My doctors and trainer helped me set goals for recovery such as a good amount of running by a certain date, which I achieved. I visualized racing in my head all the time. When I was out biking, I did it frequently. I transformed myself. I saw and heard the crowd, the announcer, other runners I know, meet directors, etc. I saw it all. I saw myself going out fast, running in the pack, hurting like in a race, saw the finish line, saw myself winning. I've always seen myself winning.

When I'm at my best physically, I always feel like I can win. In talking to other people, I don't sense that in most of them. They are finding excuses. They're already talking themselves out of doing well. I don't do that. When I'm training and I'm fit, I feel that I can win.

The mental training program this athlete designed for herself helped her recover and regain her optimum performance. It also allowed her to remain positive despite her injury: "If nothing else, this injury helped my running mentally. After overcoming injury, I could take anything anybody threw at me."

All the mental techniques discussed here are suggested in addition to seeing a medical professional. Going to the team doctor or a university health center should be the first step in healing an injury.

Healing Injuries

The following stories are examples of injured athletes who worked with me to design their own mental training programs for healing their sports injuries.

#1: Runner With a Stress Fracture

A masters athlete came to me with a long-term stress fracture. She had been training and competing with this injury for three months until the pain was too great and the fracture had begun to bleed into the surrounding muscle. The doctor had put the leg in a cast and told her not to run for six weeks. She was frustrated and angry. She was forced to accept that she was injured and had to stop her training and give up her hopes of competing in the national championships.

Her goal was to be walking at least 3 miles, three times a week, within five weeks, and to be running 10 miles a week within eight weeks. She also agreed to change these goals if she experienced continued deep pain or if the doctor found evidence of the fracture at the end of his prescribed six weeks of rest.

The athlete wrote seven affirmations for the healing of this injury on five three-by-five-inch cards and put them around her apartment and on her desk at work so she could see them several times a day. Within two weeks, she noticed how her anger began to diminish, and a real sense of control was obvious to her.

For this athlete, imagery became a time for humor and creativity. At first she saw the fracture as a jagged tear in the bone with blood running out like a waterfall. I asked her to let go of that image and to begin to see the tear healing. She reported seeing little men with bright colored threads running to the site and weaving the torn pieces together like a net. Within three weeks, she was imagining the fracture as a solid area of white like the grout between two tiles, holding firm and strong. Then I asked her to experience the bone as whole, with no lines or ridges, but smooth and healthy. She continued this program until she returned to the doctor and he gave her permission to begin running. She then began to imagine the leg being stronger than before and her body running pain free. By the end of five weeks, she was running 2 miles slowly on a bark path every other day, reporting very little pain, and she was back to her full training by the end of seven weeks.

#2: Collegiate Athlete With an Injured Hamstring

A collegiate athlete had been working on his performance and technique when he became injured with a pulled hamstring. He was a student at the local university, and he had three mid-term exams the week of his injury as well as the collegiate championships coming up in two weeks. His injury occurred at practice.

This was a recurring injury. He expressed feelings of wanting to give up, of resignation and frustration with his continued inability to stay healthy. He had planned to compete in Europe that summer and was depressed and confused.

After guiding him into a very relaxed state, I asked him to focus inside on the injured area and to ask it what it wanted from him. What was it trying to tell him? He said it wanted to rest, it wanted to be babied, to get a massage, and to be iced. It also wanted him to relax and to not stretch it too much or too hard. It did not feel listened to. He told it that he heard it, and he promised to get a massage and to be gentler. He also promised to slow down because of the stress in his life and to rest. His affirmations were "I am relaxed and creative when under stress," "I listen to my body," "I enjoy resting and caring for my body," and "My hamstrings are relaxed and flexible."

I then led him through a visualization of relaxing and healing the hamstring. After two weeks, his hamstring was healthy, and he felt a sense of freedom and control over his body and his training. He competed at top form three weeks after his injury had occurred.

#3: Recreational Athlete With a Stress Fracture

A third athlete was referred to me by her physician as a last resort. She had been injured for four and a half months with a stress fracture that had never healed. Every time she went to the doctor, the news was worse. Her ankle had been immobilized for more than two months. Surgery and a bone graft from her hip had been suggested by an orthopedic surgeon, and acupuncture had been tried unsuccessfully. Nothing was helping, and she was deeply depressed and had been sick several times. All necessary blood work had also been done, and her hormones had been checked. She was very angry and irritable and was furious with her body for not healing. She had been doing some visualizing without the help of a tape and found that her mind wandered. I asked her what she was seeing when she did these visualizations. She said she could see the broken bone as it had looked in the X ray, with only one fiber on a corner of one of the pieces connecting the separation. The bone was always broken. She had stopped the visualizations.

Her goal was to be healed and out of the brace in three weeks and to be able to go to Los Angeles on vacation. She wanted to be pain free and performing by the summer, and she wanted to learn to do healing visualizations. She also wrote two personal goals that she thought would help her body to heal. She wanted to learn to take time for herself and to let go of feeling guilty for taking that time.

The most important process for this athlete was her imagery. For four and a half months, she had been seeing the bone in her ankle broken and had been perceiving herself as injured and weak. I led her through a guided visualization that helped her to become aware of the purpose of her injury and then to experience the bone healing and whole. Instead of viewing herself as having to do everything for everyone, I asked her to experience herself doing things for herself and allowing others to be responsible for themselves. Instead of seeing the bone broken with one fiber connected on one corner, I asked her to see several fibers growing from both sides of the separation, growing toward each other and knitting together, making the bone solid and one piece. When asking the injury its purpose, she reported it was telling her to slow down, to take her time, and that she didn't have to work as hard as she had before. She continued to say things to herself such as, "I enjoy letting other people give to me," "My body is healing and becoming strong," "It is easy for me to make time for myself," and "I am comfortable nurturing myself and healing my body." A subsequent X ray one month after our first session showed the bone to be totally healed.

These three case histories demonstrate the basic issues and processes involved in dealing with athletes' reactions to injury. They also demonstrate the necessity of the athletes' involvement in the healing of their injuries. Though tangible, scientifically indisputable evidence of the mind's power to inflict damage on or heal the body is still in its infancy, research is clearly beginning to show that inner talk, imagery, and positive intent do have a powerful influence on a person's physical process. "Researchers in biofeedback have discovered that it is possible to control voluntary heart rate, muscle tension, sweat-gland activity, skin temperature and a wide range of internal physical states normally considered to be under involuntary control by the autonomic nervous system" (Matthews-Simonton, Simonton, and Creighton 1978). Just as mental imagery can produce a state of relaxation or control heart rate, mental images can enhance the speed and effectiveness of the healing process.

Athletes can communicate with their body using imagery, suggestion, and language to achieve a higher sense of control and motivation, whether for performance or healing. It is now widely accepted that athletes can use their imagination, mental pictures, and positive self-talk to make their bodies respond with peak performances in competition. This also holds true for the healing responses of the body. Training the mind to assist in the process of healing is that extra edge, the final piece that creates a whole, ultimately healthy athlete. It is the tool that athletes can use to achieve a sense of control and power when their body must rest and mend itself. Research clearly demonstrates that injury rehabilitation must include physical, mental, and emotional components to assist the athlete in regaining complete health. If you are injured, you need to

- set your own goals for recovery,
- write affirmations for healing and pain control,
- know and practice relaxation and stress reduction techniques,
- improve your concentration and focus of attention,
- write your own visualization (or use those provided in this chapter),
- be more relaxed,
- have a sense of control over your recovery,
- practice relaxation in several settings, and
- cope well with stress.

Visualizing Health

When you picture yourself well and whole, you have begun the process of creating the positive you of the future. When injured, you can visualize a time in the future when you have regained your fitness and health.

Through mental imagery, it is possible to alter the body's autonomic physiological responses. In other words, you can communicate with your body using imagery, suggestion, and language—exactly what has been described in this book. When you use your imagination, mental pictures, and suggestion, you can make your body respond.

Mental images can enhance the speed and effectiveness of the healing process. Again, you must enter as deep a state of relaxation as possible. Then create an image in your mind's eye of what you want your body to do with the injured area. The image may be highly technical, or it may be simple and imaginative. Perhaps you imagine the stress fracture site mending, the bone knitting together, blood cells surrounding the site, bringing new oxygen, replenishing and energizing the injury, and all the bad blood and wastes being removed. An energy psychology example might be visualizing rays of gold or white light surrounding the injury site, bringing warmth and healing, energizing the site and your whole body. The healing image must feel good to you and have personal significance. As with all visualizations, you should be careful to include as many visual, auditory, and kinesthetic cues as possible to create a complete and whole picture. Be specific and concrete.

I am strong, powerful, and fast.

As you visualize, think of the marked contrast between this use of imagery and your usual response to pain or illness. Too often, you probably clench your muscles, become angry, or desperately try to ignore the discomfort, hoping that aspirin or a more potent analgesic will ease the pain. Such a response makes you even more tense, creating further obstacles for your body to contend with. But in a healing visualization, you directly confront and assault the dysfunction within you by mobilizing the positive forces that can aid in the healing. Instead of passively or naively working against yourself, you actively stimulate whatever latent powers of healing lie within. You have nothing to lose and much to gain by joining in this experiment in self-healing.

Visualization for Healing

Begin to focus your attention on the injured part of your body . . . become fully aware of its depth and size and shape . . . connect completely with this injury . . . seeing it . . . hearing it . . . feeling it . . . focusing on it . . . acknowledging its presence within you . . . allow yourself to know it totally and completely . . . is it deep? . . . shallow? . . . on the surface? . . . deep inside? Connect with the injury fully . . . allow yourself to *feel* it . . . *see* it . . . *hear* it . . . be fully aware of your injured part . . . acknowledge it . . . know it . . .

When you are fully aware of the injured part, ask it what it is trying to tell you . . . what does it need from you? Listen to what it says . . . what does it want from you and what does it want you to do? . . . listen carefully . . . when it is finished, thank it for its message . . .

After you have thanked it for its message, begin to allow yourself to forgive this injury . . . letting go of any anger, hate, or frustration you may have felt for it . . . allowing yourself to forgive it . . . to let go . . . to release any negative energy you may have been feeling for the injury . . . send it forgiveness . . . letting go of any resistance you have had for it . . . softening . . . releasing . . . dispersing any negativity into the shape of a small ball . . . see it float away . . . out of your sight . . .

Slowly begin to send loving and healing energy to the injury . . . visualizing energy flowing down from the universe into your body . . . releasing the tightness and the resistance in your body . . . sending it into the ground beneath your feet . . .

imagine and feel the muscle tissue around the injury relaxing . . . softening . . . releasing . . . imagine the injury healing . . . getting stronger and stronger . . . imagine all the blood coursing through your arteries bringing new food and oxygen to the hurt . . . taking away the injured cells . . . new healthy cells taking their place . . . revitalizing those sore and tender parts . . . the new blood healing the tissue or the bone . . . circulating around the injury . . . building new tissue . . . caressing the injured part until it is well and healthy again . . .

Send the injury loving energy for all the times it has come through for you in the past . . . be patient with it . . . knowing it needs some time to heal . . . telling it you love it . . . releasing any animosity or anger you might have for it . . . feel the energy from the universe above you flowing through your body, releasing any and all heavy energy within you, replacing it with a lighter feeling of health and well-being . . .

Begin giving the injured area a healing color . . . a beautiful royal blue . . . an emerald green . . . a pale golden color . . . the warm color bathing the injured area . . . healing it . . . loving it . . . remembering the love you have in your heart for someone special, feel that love in your heart and body now, and begin to connect with this openhearted loving energy . . . allow yourself to send that same feeling of love to your injured part . . . easily . . . gently . . . send warmth and love to this area . . . letting go and softening around the injury . . . telling it how much it means to you and how much you appreciate the work it has done for you in the past . . . send it love . . . send it peace . . . send it healing . . . send it warmth . . . letting go of any fear that surrounds it . . . allow yourself to release any tightness you might still feel around the injured part . . . setting it free . . . softly . . . gently let your body be soft and open . . . forgiving and loving . . .

Begin to focus again on the soft . . . warm . . . peaceful area of your body, which is now healing . . . send it strength . . . send it energy . . . send it love . . . imagine a pale golden color surrounding the injured area . . . see it and feel it expanding from the injured area into all parts of your body . . . the warm golden color beginning to bathe your body in its light . . . beginning at the top of your head . . . flowing down through your neck . . . chest . . . into your arms . . . hands . . . fingers

... through your abdomen ... stomach ... into your legs ... feet ... and toes ... see and feel yourself filled with a warm, golden yellow light ... the color filling your body ... filling it with love and energy ... you are healing ...

See and feel the injury becoming flexible ... strong ... supple ... remembering the healing ... knowing your body will come through for you ... restoring you to good health ... again being in an energetic ... vibrant state ... full of endurance and good health ... see and feel yourself performing at your peak ... happy ... lively ... fulfilled and content ... imagine healing Mother Earth energy flowing up through your body from your feet and the base of your spine ... again filling your body with a soothing feeling of lightness and healing ... imagine the two flows of energy from the universe and Mother Earth flowing in parallel flows within your body ... they meet in your solar plexus (two inches above your navel) and flow in a strong, powerful stream out of your solar plexus region and into the air in front of you ... you feel strong, powerful, and centered ... remembering and saying to yourself some affirmations for healing, "I am healing and healed ... My body is healthy and strong ... I am healing quickly ... I am healthier every day ... I am healthy and pain free ... I care for and nurture my body ... My body part is strong, flexible, and healthy ... I am completely healed ... I am performing at my peak ... ."

Know that you have everything within you to be, do, and have what it is that you want ... You are healing and healed ... you love your body ... you are whole ... Begin to reconnect with your present space now ... bring your focus to your breathing ... the sounds of the room ... the feel of your body against the chair or the couch ... remember that you are healing and becoming healthy and whole ... thank your body as you reconnect with its sensations and the space around you ... after counting to three you may open your eyes ... refreshed ... relaxed ... alert ... healthy and at peace ... one ... move your fingers and toes ... becoming aware of the sounds and your breathing ... two ... move your head, shoulders, and back ... feeling soft and relaxed ... three ... open your eyes when you are ready.

Visualization for Pain Control

Begin to focus your attention on the area of pain within your body . . . become fully aware of its depth and size and shape . . . connect completely with this pain . . . facing it directly . . . centering on it . . . focusing on it . . . acknowledging its presence within you . . . allow yourself to know it totally and completely . . . notice its temperature . . . is it hot, cold, cool, warm? . . . is it deep? . . . shallow? . . . is it sharp or dull? . . . be aware if it is constant or if it comes and goes . . . connect with the pain fully . . . allow yourself to *feel* it . . . see it . . . hear it . . . moment to moment . . . notice if it has a color . . . if it does, focus on that color . . . is the color dark or light? Does the color intensify or diminish the pain? Be aware now . . . in the present . . . acknowledge it . . . know it . . . feel it . . . see it . . .

Now that you are fully aware of it, ask the pain what it is trying to tell you . . . what message does it have for you? Listen to what it says . . . what does it want from you and what is it trying to give to you? Listen carefully . . . when it is finished, thank it for its message . . . after you have thanked it for its message, begin to allow yourself to forgive this pain . . . letting go of any anger, hate, or frustration you may have felt for it . . . allowing yourself to forgive it . . . to let go . . . to release any negative energy you may have been feeling in regard to the pain . . . send it forgiveness . . . letting go of any resistance you have had for it . . . softening . . . releasing . . . dispersing any negativity into the shape of a small cloud . . . see it drift away, out of your sight.

Slowly begin to soften around the pain now . . . letting go . . . releasing the tightness and the resistance in your body . . . imagine the muscle tissue around the pain relaxing . . . melting . . . softening . . . releasing . . . allow the pain to melt like butter . . . becoming smooth . . . give it a healing color now . . . a beautiful royal blue . . . an emerald green . . . a pale gold color . . . any color you choose . . .

Imagine a person whom you love very much . . . see this person's face before you . . . feel the love in your heart for this person . . . connect with the openhearted loving energy in your heart, and begin to allow yourself to send the love you feel in your heart to the pain in your body . . . easily . . . gently . . . send warmth and love to this area . . . letting go and softening around the pain . . . send it healing . . . send it warmth . . . letting go . . . releasing . . . freeing the pain from the area it has lived in and allowing it to float freely, soft, smooth . . . light . . . release any fear that surrounds it . . . allow yourself to release the tightness that holds it . . . setting it free . . . softly . . . gently . . . let your body be soft and open . . . forgiving the pain and loving your body . . .

Now begin to visualize the pain getting smaller and smaller . . . be aware of its shape as it floats free and becomes fainter . . . smaller . . . lighter . . . let it grow dim and smaller . . . smaller until it begins to float away from your body . . . release it . . . let it go . . . out of your body . . . out of your mind . . . out of your awareness and into the air . . . tiny . . . floating . . . away into the mist . . . gone . . .

Focus again on the soft . . . warm . . . peaceful area of your body . . . sending it healing and strength . . . sending it love and energy . . . you are pain free . . . you have let go and moved into your softness and into your healing . . . allowing yourself to rest . . . thanking your body for its strength and its willingness to release the pain . . . see and feel yourself as free of pain . . . rest into your healing . . . your body and mind harmonious . . . quiet and at peace . . .

Begin to reconnect with your present space now . . . bring your focus to your breathing . . . the sounds of the room . . . the feel of your body against the chair or the floor . . . remember that you are pain free and whole . . . thank your body as you reconnect with its sensations and the space around you . . . counting to three you may open your eyes . . . refreshed . . . relaxed . . . alert, healthy, and at peace . . .

One . . . move your fingers and toes . . . becoming aware of the sounds and your breathing . . . two . . . move your head and shoulders . . . feeling soft and gentle . . . three . . . open your eyes when you are ready.

In all of these techniques, you choose how you wish to cope with your injury or pain. This book does not advocate that you perform with pain. These methods are for you to use in managing and dealing with pain from athletic activity and injury. Each technique is based on the general mental training program or positive self-thoughts and visualizations. You must send energy, light, and love to your injured or painful body part, and you must regard it as a friend to be helped and healed rather than an enemy to be resented or feared. When you want to eliminate the problem, it helps to tell the body part it is loved and that you wish for it to be healed so that it can assist you in your athletic performance.

Simple affirmations such as, "I am healthy," "I am healing rapidly," "I am healed," and "My body is repairing itself perfectly" will allow your mind to assist in the healing process your body is attempting and help bring about a rapid recovery. Seeing yourself healed and healthy is the first step on your journey to recovery.

Coaching Young Athletes

In my work with younger athletes, I noticed many of them had similar issues, regardless of what sport they played. The following list represents the main issues of young athletes:

- Focus and concentration
- Learning to visualize
- Stopping negative self-talk
- Controlling anger on the field or court
- Precompetition anxiety and fear
- What other people think of them

Actually, many of the adults reading this chapter will probably say, "Those are my issues too!" and they may well be. Younger athletes sometimes haven't learned yet how to deal with self-doubt, peer pressure, or authority. After you have been functioning in the world for a while, you learn to deal with some of these things, but there is still a part of you that struggles with these issues.

The mental training process doesn't change when it is applied to coaching a young athlete. The chapters of this book describe the processes to use for addressing the issues of young athletes. Topics such as learning to visualize and positive self-talk are covered in chapters 4 and 6. Dealing with anger and fear can be found in chapter 8. The main difference in a program tailored toward young athletes is that, as a coach, you must break their learning down into smaller chunks.

Remember, though, that no one can be forced to learn this process. Young athletes must be willing to change and to do something different in order to create the space for improvement. If you, as a coach, are supportive of mental training, other team members will listen.

Before her fourth grand-slam win in 1998 at the Australian Open, 17-year-old Martina Hingis said, "I'm probably mentally stronger and more self-confident than I was last year. To defend the title is much harder than coming here for the first time when nobody expected me to win" (Wilstein 1998). That year, Hingis became the youngest player in the Open era to defend a grand-slam title.

Now is the time for young athletes to learn how to do mental training. Using mental training is a matter of exposure and awareness. It's okay to go slow in implementing a mental training program. Some athletes will love it, and some of your athletes, maybe even the ones who you think would benefit most, will never touch it. As coach, you need great measures of patience, tolerance, and acceptance in this process.

Martina Hingis, the youngest player to win a Grand Slam in tennis, is mentally tough and self-confident.

© SportsChrome

Tailoring Training

One of the best ways to improve your players' concentration is to have them listen to a 10- to 15-minute guided visualization using headphones, while sitting with their eyes closed in a quiet room. This mental focus on listening to a voice and imagining visual and physical responses to their sport teaches them to focus and refocus constantly. People's minds wander constantly, grasping at each new idea or thought that comes up. Listening to guided visualizations brings your athletes' attention to one spot, and they will learn to mentally track for longer and longer periods of time. Before they learn to track, they must be willing to surrender to doing *nothing* but sitting and listening for 10 to 15 minutes—without going to sleep. That's discipline in itself!

Use visualization and imagery practice three to four times a week with your team to help them imagine playing their positions as well as they'd like to play them—doing things right, having a lot of speed, having good energy, having strength and endurance, and really putting themselves out there.

If they have trouble focusing, the process can be facilitated by having the athletes practice a breathing technique where they hold their right index finger over their right nostril, breathing through their left nostril for 30 seconds to a minute. This accesses the right brain, slows down left-brain thinking, stops mind chatter, and facilitates right-brain processing. If the athletes are between 8 and 13, an even shorter visualization time period is recommended, perhaps 10 minutes or less at the beginning. Also, when teaching them the mental training program, sessions should be no longer than 30 to 45 minutes each. Keep them interested and on target, in simple and short segments.

When the athletes are tired or down, you should use positive self-talk and affirmations such as "I'm strong," "I'm fast," and "I'm powerful" to get them going. You should also talk more, encouraging team members and congratulating them on good shots and good plays. Encourage them to do the same for each other. When using a mental training program for young athletes, be sure to always have them do the following:

- Analyze their game to identify what they did right.
- Acknowledge themselves for doing it right.
- Analyze what they did wrong and work on it during the next week's practice.

- Try to let go of a loss and focus on the next game coming up.
- Practice more "intensity" shots under pressure in practice. (Practice with people "in your face," not every day, but for a day or two to try different things and to see what works and what doesn't.)

Working With Parents

On the sidelines or in the stands, probably since the beginning of sports history, there have been parents who were enthusiastic, supportive, critical, loving, pushing, caring, and demanding. Most of the time, the attitude of the parents is crucial to the athletic performance, good or bad, of the child. After working with young athletes, their parents, and coaches, I was asked to come up with a list of what works and what doesn't for the parents of aspiring young athletes. I would advise you, as a coach, to use this list or modify it if you see fit. Give it to all the parents of your athletes at the beginning of each season.

Most children play sports because they have fun playing. When sports become work and drudgery, children lose interest, and they lose some of the joy in growing up. Remembering to be a little less serious about life can help everybody enjoy athletic competition. This simple list may help parents to remember that youth sports are to be enjoyed by children as well as parents. The following are the most powerful dos and don'ts for parents who want to support their children in the most positive and beneficial way.

The Dos

- Allow your children to be interested in and want to play whatever sport they choose. Provide the opportunity for them to consider many choices, and support their choice even if it is not yours. If a child is most comfortable with the choice to play no sport, support that choice.
- Teach your children to respect their coach. Do this primarily by showing respect to the coach yourself. For children to make progress and improve their performance, it is vital that they listen to and trust the coach's advice and instructions.
- Be willing to let your children make their own mistakes and learn from them. When your children make mistakes, ask what they think they could have done differently, what they learned from the experience, and if they would like any feedback from

you. If they do, your feedback should be what you saw, what you think they might have done differently, and what you think they might have learned (not criticism or blame).

- Be interested and supportive, light and playful, understanding and openhearted. Be accepting and tolerant of your children's learning process and their physical abilities. Acknowledge and enjoy your children's participation and successes, even the small ones.
- Model flexibility of your own opinions. Be willing to be wrong and move off your position. Listen to the other side of the situation and let go of the need to be right or in control.

The Don'ts

- Don't try to relive your youth through your children. Just because you were, or wanted to be, a hero on the football field or in gymnastics does not mean that your children will choose to play *that* sport. Accept that your children may not excel in that or any sport.
- Don't blame the equipment, the coach, other players, the referees, or even the weather if your child or the team does not do well or win. Blaming others teaches nonaccountability to kids. They do not learn to look at what they could have done differently, or learn from their mistakes, if they learn to blame others.
- Don't push, push, push. Children who are pushed beyond their capabilities may lose their self-confidence, become resistant and resentful toward their parent, become unsure of themselves and their abilities, and may stop trying. They may also exhibit a disturbance in eating or sleeping habits.
- Don't expect perfection or tie your ego or image to your child's performance. Perfectionism is a very hard expectation to live up to. Laying guilt on a child because her performance made *you* look bad is highly destructive. Your child is *not* responsible for your ego or your reputation in the community.

Carl Lewis and Mary Decker Slaney are two of the greatest American runners of all time, and they each dominated their events in the '70s, '80s, and into the '90s. Carl Lewis won a total of eight gold medals in four Olympics, and Mary Slaney held at one time almost every American record in middle and longer distances. Mary became a nationally known runner at the age of

14, and she has outrun and outlasted all of her contemporaries from the '70s, '80s, and '90s. In 1980, she set a record of 4:00.8 in the 1500 meters, a mark that stood for two decades.

These two runners both had extraordinary talent when they were young, and they were both able to compete well into their late thirties at the international level. Many young athletes are hot flames, which soon burn out; but it is possible, with care and balanced training, for an athlete who starts young to compete successfully for many years.

Tiger Woods, as a young golf phenomenon, won the U.S. Amateur tournament three times. He was the leading money winner his first year on the PGA tour, winning four tournaments, including the U.S. Masters with an unbelievable 18 under par. He finished second and third in two other tournaments.

Tiger revitalized the golf industry with his powerful mental abilities, combined with his incredible talent and youthful appeal. He began playing at three and was winning junior tournaments at five or six.

All three of these athletes have diverse backgrounds from each other; but in each case, they had adult mentors or parents who supported them emotionally, mentally, and physically. All three have powerful focus and concentration abilities to go with their supreme talents in their sport. They are all inspirations to the young people who follow their athletic feats and hold them in high esteem.

A young Oregon athlete also exemplifies the use of mental training and visualization in his competitions.

Chris Sprague saw the dream throw many times in his mind the last week before Oregon's Centennial Relays. On Saturday he saw it in reality as the junior from South Eugene High School smashed the state's 22-year-old record for the shot put with the best series of throws ever by an Oregon prep during the Centennial Relays.

"I didn't touch the weights for a week and did a lot of visualization," he said after establishing a state standard with a mark of 65-5. "I thought about it before going to bed every night. I just wanted to get a good throw, and it happened."

Sprague also had the longest throw in the discus, hitting a personal best of 181-7 to beat last year's state champion Mark Hoxmeier of Hillsboro and erase the meet record of 179-9 by Brian Crouser of Gresham in 1980.

The record in the shot came on his first throw in the finals—one of his three marks beyond the 65-foot stripe and the old state record of 64-9 by Curt Denny in 1975. The meet record was 60-11 by Edger Mitchell of Central Catholic in 1982.

Sprague said Denny's former coach at Burns, Cal Garrison, congratulated him after the meet. "He asked if I used visualization," Sprague said of his conversation with Garrison. "I told him that I did, and he said most of the good ones do." (RGN 1997)

Not all young athletes are as talented as the ones described here, but there are things parents can do to facilitate their children's budding athletic careers and help their children enjoy the years that they compete. The list of dos and don'ts for parents is a good start.

Being Female

"It's not feminine to sweat . . . to be a good athlete . . . to be aggressive . . . to beat the boys or men . . . " When it comes to being athletes, women have been conditioned by society to believe they are mentally and physically inferior to men. Because the attributes that lead to athletic success—determination, aggressiveness, leadership, competitiveness, self-confidence—are generally considered masculine, the need to adhere to an acceptably feminine role has discouraged women from participating in sports. Women are taught that they are not strong enough or fast enough or mentally tough enough to be great athletes.

At what age do women learn to stop competing and start limiting themselves to save someone else's ego or to fit into their peer group? Boys are expected to participate in sports and are actually pushed by their fathers and peers to be athletic. This will bring them validation and reward. Young girls are urged to be "little ladies" and are usually recognized and rewarded for feminine pursuits related to house and family. In college, many girls lower their self-expectations and ambitions to avoid the disapproval of their male peers, who may feel threatened by too much competence and ambition in a woman. "Independence, aggressiveness and competitive achievement, all of which may threaten the success of heterosexual relationships, are often given up by adolescent girls in order to increase their attractiveness to boys" (Bardwick and Douvan 1972). Unfortunately, even in the 21st century, this is still true for many women, young or old. Not surprisingly then,

I am an aggressive player who makes plays happen.

female athletes have special needs in the area of sport psychology and mental training. They need to overcome the negative programming and self-talk that they have internalized since childhood.

Swimmer Amy Van Dyken won four gold medals in the Olympics in Atlanta in 1996, and in recognition of her accomplishment, was voted the USOC Sports Woman of the Year. Van Dyken's Olympic appearance, which began with disappointment, a fourth place finish in the 100-meters freestyle, had suddenly turned into a historic achievement. She was the first U.S. female athlete to win four gold medals at a single Olympic games.

Conquering disappointment was nothing new for Van Dyken. She had overcome childhood asthma and some early struggles to get to the top of the medal stand in Atlanta. The smiling Amy, with the four gold medals was, after all, the same swimmer whose high school teammates had once refused to swim with, "because I was so bad," she said. And she's the same swimmer who quit the sport for a time in 1993 after a bout of mononucleosis. (Zang 1997)

The age when a female athlete begins to hold herself back and mold herself according to the expectations of society and her peers depends on the individual. It is exciting to find that in the younger generations, many girls are willing to forge ahead, to fly in the face of outdated concepts to perform at their highest level. They are willing to take risks to reach their peak athletic performances, as everybody must be willing to do. As a female athlete, what are some of your issues and concerns? Use Mental Trainer #10 to write down these issues and identify how these issues help or hinder you.

Acting Aggressively

Aggressiveness is learned most easily by pushing yourself to act aggressively even if it feels uncomfortable at first. This does not

Mental Trainer #10:   Female, Athletic, and Proud

My female athletic issue is:

Does it help me or hinder me?
How?

My female athletic issue is:

Does it help me or hinder me?
How?

My female athletic issue is:

Does it help me or hinder me?
How?

mean being obnoxious, loud, or cocky. Aggressiveness means asserting yourself, being an initiator, being proactive rather than reactive (that is, rather than simply responding to someone else's initiative or move). Rushing the net, going for a rebound, surging in a race, and intercepting a shot are all examples of assertive and aggressive behavior. You are merely initiating a play or move instead of waiting to respond.

You can be aggressive without being hostile or angry. Many coaches resort to making their players angry to arouse their energy and aggression. This works to a certain extent because the players go into the challenge mode of "I'll show *you!*" The athletes become champions not because of an "okayness" in their mind, but because of an attitude of "I'll prove myself to you," and "I'm right, you're wrong." There are times when this may work, but this technique often backfires when athletes are under pressure. When the pressure gets too great, anger is not enough, and the athletes lose mental control and focus. There is nothing left to rely on. Often as a result the team chokes or the athletes tighten and lose their rhythm.

Dealing with anger is a crucial issue for all athletes, both male and female, but females especially are often uncomfortable being angry or having someone angry with them. Women are not used to conflict or confrontation. They are taught that their anger is unacceptable and unladylike. Women can learn that it is as acceptable for them as it is for men to feel and express their anger and frustration when in competition.

The objective for dealing with anger is to be the master of your emotions, to acknowledge the feelings and then drop them, refocusing on the task at hand and staying in the present moment. Letting go and dropping the anger you feel is crucial in becoming a great athlete.

Mary Decker Slaney felt anger, frustration, and pain when she fell during the finals for the gold medal in the 3000-meter race at the 1984 Olympics. She said later that if she had been much more aggressive and pushed back while she was in the pack, that she most likely wouldn't have fallen. Extreme emotions are natural to all humans, especially in highly stressful situations. An athlete shouldn't put forth a display of emotion that destroys her focus and eventually her performance. But she should be aware of all her emotions, acknowledge their existence, and use constructive control—being aggressive if she needs to be.

Competing Against Friends

Competing with and beating their friends and teammates seems to be a real concern for young college women. I interviewed an outstanding national-class runner, and I was fascinated by her story about an important race with a teammate:

> We were running together and I was in front, leading most of the way. She kept surging to pass me and every time she got even with me, I picked up the pace so she couldn't pass. This happened several times and on the last homestretch, I kicked and won. I felt terrible about it and apologized to her afterward. She didn't seem to mind, but it made me very uncomfortable because she was my friend and I didn't want her to be angry with me.

I discussed with her this fear of hurting or angering her friend. I reframed the race for her and told her to look at it from a different perspective: "You are here to compete and you were being fair. This is the whole idea of competition. Your friend wanted to win too and that is what she was trying to do. Both of you were pulling and pushing each other to run, helping each other to achieve a peak performance, to run better and faster." She agreed with this perspective and went on to the best performances of her college career, setting numerous personal records in her event all season and in Europe. She became a fine competitor, aggressive yet controlled and fair, optimizing her substantial talent and ability. She brought her mental ability up to par with her physical ability.

Taking Time for Yourself

Women have long been taught to be caregivers to others. For women age 25 and older, taking time for themselves is often felt to be selfish, not only by their family, but by the women themselves. These feelings come from the belief that the family should come first. However, research has shown that the more people nurture themselves, the more care and nurturing they can give to others. This self-care helps restore the internal energy system of the person. It "fills up the well" so that more love and energy can be given to others.

Activities that furnish a woman with athletic success enhance her self-concept and confidence. Athletic training and competition help develop a sense of accomplishment and can be an excellent opportunity for the family to return some of the support and love they have received.

When a female parent becomes athletic, many families put pressure on her to stay at home more to meet the family's needs. A subtle underlying guilt trip from the family may undermine athletic desire and achievement. Dealing with this attitude can be difficult. The more a family gives back love and support, the more the female athlete will be able to perform at her best without distraction. Support from the family, such as allowing guilt-free training time, attending competitions, and assuming some of the responsibilities at home can do wonders in creating family unity and pride. If a woman communicates honestly with her family about how important it is to her that they support her athletic participation, this can help build an enduring and broad base of family harmony.

Worrying About Others

While interviewing female athletes from team and individual sports, I learned of another major performance issue. Many women had problems with their concentration and focus because they were so concerned with what the audience or coach was thinking about them. Gymnasts and tennis players often had this problem. They were self-conscious and worried about how they looked when performing. They were concerned about their acceptability as compared to someone else. They were concerned about making a fool of themselves and losing face.

The moment any athlete shifts mental focus from self to others, concentration is lost. Most women are not self-focused. They have learned that it is more acceptable to be outwardly focused, to be concerned about the other person. Loss of concentration results in missed shots or falling off the beam or loss of rhythm and form. This problem is widespread among athletes who must perform solo. (It is not so prevalent in team sports where the group energy and group identity help an individual melt into the team image.) By focusing on her form or routine, the female athlete can eliminate this problem and improve her concentration.

Another concern of female athletes has to do with other people thinking they are gay or homosexual because they are a "jock." Many coaches and athletes are so fearful of people thinking they are gay that they adopt homophobic responses. One coach was so concerned with his team's feminine image that he would not publicly allow his team to be associated with any sports professionals who he had heard were gay or bisexual. This is a sad situation, not only because it perpetuates the paranoia, but also because it robs a team of skilled professional services. Should an athlete happen to be gay, he or she might live in fear of being found out while working with a coach who displays this attitude.

It is acceptable to be feminine and a fine athlete, and it should also be acceptable to be a fine athlete and set your own standards of femininity. The female athlete should nurture a strong sense of power, personal identity, and self-confidence. Part of a coach's job is to promote and support these psychological characteristics in athletes. Sexual orientation has very little connection with athletic performance and should be left to an athlete's personal discretion.

Treating Eating Disorders

Eating disorders, mainly anorexia and bulimia, occur all too often in the sporting world. Many articles and books have been written about these disorders—their frequency, their purported causes, and possible treatments. The reality is, at the current time, they are difficult to treat, and no one really knows exactly what causes people, athletes and nonathletes, to become anorexic or bulimic. Approximately 90 percent of people with eating disorders are female. There are many theories about the causes of eating disorders, most of which seem to be only theories; no hard proof has yet come in. The important thing to know is what to do about eating disorders.

All stages of eating disorders are deeply affected by a negative mind-set that tells the person that she is unworthy of eating, love, and anything nurturing or worthwhile. People with eating disorders seem to be at war with themselves and seem to have two minds: their actual mind and a powerful negative mind. When the eating disorder is present, the negative mind is totally in control, turning self-doubt, indecisiveness, and self-criticism into unbridled self-destruction.

Eating disorders are an important problem that is often swept under the table by coaches who feel incompetent and helpless about what to do for their athletes. Some of the more unhelpful practices of coaches have been group weigh-ins, weight goals, remarks about "looking a little heavy," and associating weight loss with enhanced performance. One of the better articles describing eating disorder issues of athletes is the chapter "Eating Disorders and Weight Management in Athletes," by Robert A. Swoap, PhD, and Shane Murphy, PhD, in the excellent book, *Sport Psychology Interventions* (1995). Murphy is the former director of the U.S. Olympic Committee's sport psychology program. The chapter is a comprehensive overview of the problems and issues of restricting weight, performance demands, and coach pressure on athletes to stay thin and trim. Even in this well-done article of 23 pages, only 6 pages offer recommendations for treatment and prevention. The truth is everybody knows it is a big problem, and most people don't know what to do about it!

Reviving Ophelia (2002) by Mary Pipher, PhD, is an important book that examines the dangers of being a young female in American society, and it provides suggestions on how adults can help. The book has stories and examples that examine the pressures facing young American women to be beautiful, sophisticated, and thin. Eye opening and frank, this book is a must-read for adults who work with young female athletes.

Eating disorders are hard to treat and often hard to detect, in the general population and in athletes. There is no easy solution, but early detection is a good prognosis for recovery. Athletes who have eating disorders need to find a good therapist to help them deal with these issues. Good counseling is essential to recovery.

As you may already know, there are many books about food, diet, nutrition, and eating disorders. One fascinating book is *When Food Is Love* (1991) by Geneen Roth. Roth draws parallels between intimacy and eating, and she truly sees the patterns of why many women, and some men, eat excessively. Basically, Roth feels that people eat to nurture themselves and to protect themselves from vulnerability, that is, intimacy. Does that ring true for you? How many times have you eaten something delicious to satisfy some longing or need deep inside you? Chocolate is a favorite food because in addition to tasting good, it creates endorphins in the brain, and endorphins create feelings of pleasure and well-being. In her book, Roth talks about intimacy and why it is so frightening to many people:

> Intimacy is showing another person the parts of ourselves that we believe to be unworthy and thereby risking that they will turn from us the way our parents did. (A voice inside screams: "It was excruciating the first time and now you're asking me to go through it again?") Intimacy brings with it tenderness and humor, companionship and affection, but it also demands that we relive the most agonizing moments of being a child.

The significance of giving up the obsession with food is not a thinner body, not a smaller pants size, but giving up your protection from pain, for when you protect yourself from pain, you protect yourself from intimacy. When you allow your pain to be visible, you can give it a voice. And when you give it a voice, you can release yourself from it.

The first step in healing is telling the truth. When you tell the truth, you acknowledge your losses. When you acknowledge your losses, you grieve about them. When you grieve about them, you let go of defining yourself by how much and how badly you've been abused. You begin living in the present instead of living in reaction to the past.

Compulsive eating is a symbolic reenactment of the way in which we distorted our feelings when we began eating compulsively; we swallowed our feelings; we blamed ourselves; we felt out of control; we believed we couldn't get enough. If we allow ourselves to get sidetracked into believing that food is our problem, we will never heal the wounds that we became compulsive to express.

Compulsive eaters want the longing to be stilled. The small child within is ignored by us, as she was ignored by her parents. We substitute the longing to be thin for the longing for love.

Geneen Roth speaks the truth. You have waited long enough. You, as a woman, have given enough of yourself away. It is time to feel and to be complete. Healing your child and loving every aspect of yourself gives you the courage and ability to love and accept others, to stop the separation of self and others, and to close the gap of separation and loneliness. In learning to trust yourself, you learn to trust others. You, as an athlete and a woman, need to take control of your own life and not rely on others to "save you" or to make things happen for you.

Compulsive overeating and undereating both represent hidden psychological issues that need to be explored and healed. A competent therapist who specializes in eating disorders can be of immense help in overcoming long-standing food and weight issues.

If you think you have an eating disorder, you must find a good program or therapist to work with. It is easier to handle and conquer this problem when you have the help and support of a professional. Give yourself permission to ask for help and assistance. It is never a sign of weakness to ask; it is a sign of caring and self-nurturing to let others help you.

Working with food issues is different and sometimes more difficult than other issues because eating is not a habit people want to stop, like smoking, drug abuse, and so forth. In the right combinations and amounts, food nourishes the body. People depend on eating to survive. Even if you do not have any eating issues, you should take some time to look at your eating patterns and the food you consistently eat. What is your intake of caffeine, sugar, fat, and processed foods? Do you drink pure or filtered water? Do you eat or drink as few chemicals as possible (that is, boxed or prepackaged meals and food items)? Do you eat organic vegetables and fruits? Do you know where your chicken has been and how it was raised? Additives and hormones given to chickens, pigs, and cattle for rapid growth play dangerous games with your body's hormonal levels and can seriously affect your athletic performance.

Playing for Yourself

One issue coaches talk about has to do with motivating the female athlete to work hard and to take her performance or the team's performance seriously. For reasons that are not well understood, some coaches of team sports have a difficult time motivating their athletes, getting the athletes to practice as hard as they need to if they are to beat more "upbeat" teams. Coaches are frequently frustrated trying to figure out how to get their players to play hard and aggressively. Why athletes play is an important issue. They may be playing for the wrong reasons and therefore pulling down team morale.

Those athletes who succeed at the highest levels play for the sheer love of it. It is what they want to do. But many women play for other reasons, and you must be aware of these reasons if you wish to perform and compete at your highest level. Here are some of those other reasons:

- To impress somebody (my father or parents, my brother, my boyfriend).
- To keep my scholarship and stay in school.
- To keep my weight down.
- Fear of rejection by somebody (my coach, my father or parents, my peers).
- To avoid being judged as a sissy.

Take a look at your own motivation. Why are you an athlete, and why do you work hard to do your best and to compete at your highest level? Use Mental Trainer #11 to help you become aware of what motivates you to play your sport.

Mental Trainer #11:   Motivators

My sport:

Why I compete (in order of importance):

1. _____

2. _____

3. _____

4. _____

5. _____

6. _____

How I feel about my sport and my reasons:

When I work with teams and individuals who are confronting a motivation problem, anger and frustration between the athletes and the coach or between team members often surface. I encourage the athletes and coaches to share their concerns, needs, and fears in open-minded, honest communication sessions. I act as a facilitator for this process. Their willingness to put themselves in a position of vulnerability with one another usually clears the air for all concerned. This allows energies to be focused on performance and competition rather than personal issues. I have experienced a lot of success using this method of conflict resolution. The achievements and motivation of the teams that participated have grown and expanded.

Regardless of the many issues faced by women athletes—the old-fashioned beliefs about femininity, other peoples' judgments, concern over beating a friend, difficulty giving themselves permission to train and achieve—they can compete knowing the following are true:

- It is okay to be a woman and a champion.
- Women are strong enough and fast enough to be outstanding athletes.
- A woman can be beautiful, feminine, and a great athlete.
- Your personal self-concept is all that matters.
- Being physically active and fit is healthy, acceptable, and desirable in today's world.

Aging Female Athletes

A study that I conducted a few years ago on women runners showed that women between the ages of 30 and 60 use running as a coping skill to deal with frustration and tension, and to increase relaxation. Although the majority did not report using running for relief of depression, they did report that when they were not able to run for periods of a week or two (due to illness or other factors) they became depressed and irritable.

The vast majority did not enjoy running as beginners, but after they had increased their mileage to five or six miles per run, they began to enjoy the benefits. They recommended going on a run when you are feeling tense and frustrated.

All in all, the total group of women used running for physical activity, for improving body image, for weight control, and for relaxation purposes. As a result, they seemed more comfortable with their own aging process. Much of the psychological benefit for women over 35 was improved body image. They liked their bodies. How many women over 40 or 50 do you know who don't like their bodies? I had a terrible time with aging when I was younger. When I was 29, I thought it was the end of the world. When I turned 30, I thought I was supposed to become a matron! That has changed for thousands of women. Now they think, "Oh boy, a new age division!"

And, as women age, into their 50s and 60s, their thoughts now are, *I can still run four to six miles and feel good. Thank you, body, for your health and fitness. I am grateful to be alive and happy in this beautiful world!*

In retrospect, years after this study, it becomes clear that it was the beginning of the running boom, and it was the "baby boomers" who were running. Now, in the 21st century, hundreds of women are taking to the streets again, this time to walk! I am currently training women over 40 to walk the Portland Marathon. It takes longer than running, but it is still as satisfying to the mind and the body. The motto of a popular walking group for women in Portland, Oregon, is *"I am an athlete!"* Indeed! Barriers of all types for women in athletics are being broken daily.

You may find other needs in your athletic life where you want to apply the tools of mental training. The next chapter focuses on applying mental training methods to life situations.

Chapter 10

Mental Training for Life

If we are not the body, what are we? If we are not the mind, what are we? If we are the spirit, what is that? Does our spirit go on?

Research indicates that future success emanates totally and absolutely from a person's present mental attitude and self-concept. If you have accepted, as previously discussed, that the pictures in your mind—how you see yourself, your self-concept—have real and actual power, you can understand the importance of those pictures. If, in your mind, you see yourself as unacceptable in your peer group, your relationships, or your workplace, you will eventually manifest this in reality.

What is mind? It is that thinking part of yourself—the visions, the thoughts, the dreams—the part of you that talks to itself, analyzing, creating, thinking. It is the part of you that separates you from the "lower animals." In any case, it is the part of you that is responsible for creativity, thinking, and problem solving. Combining the mind with the heart, or "thinking with your heart," allows you to balance the analytical part of yourself with the emotional, feeling part. You can change your mind through the use of powerful affirmations because they help you recondition your thinking and reframe your experiences into a positive, learning mode. This allows you to create a new reality for yourself with your mind and your emotions.

And what of spirit? The spirit knows at the deepest level who you are: that you are perfect as you are now, that you deserve love and respect, that you are special and gifted in some way, and that you are different from all others (and that that is where your beauty lies). The spirit is not something you think about. It serves you best when you quiet yourself and when you are willing to move your mind aside and listen to the still, small voice inside. Your spirit knows without a doubt that you are strong, that you are acceptable and perfect, and that you have the power to do and to have anything you want. In fact, it is your spirit that deeply wants you to experience your peak ability in everything you do. But your mind would have you think differently. Your mind tells you to be afraid, to doubt yourself, to compare your abilities with those of others, and to judge or to quit. Your mind wants to be in control so you give it the greatest power. So also, then, you must train it to work for you and not against you. You must also assist your mind to trust your spirit.

In the 21st century, more and more people are unwilling to accept a way of life bound by the mind and its fears and judgments. People want more. They want to change and to know and trust their spirits and true knowing. How do you get what you want when it comes to changing your internal world and your life in general?

Getting What You Want Out of Life

Whether or not you allow yourself to have what you want is based on your level of self-acceptance. If you believe you deserve to have what you want, you will go toward the accomplishment of that goal. If, on the other hand, you do not accept yourself, and you feel there is something lacking, something to be ashamed of, or something less than perfect about yourself, you will deny yourself the things you wish for. The self-acceptance you are not giving yourself is based on your judgment of yourself as not measuring up to some standard that you hold. You also use this standard to judge others. People are their own worst critics. That is why people are so hurt or angry when someone criticizes or judges them. The critics are saying what the person is already feeling or thinking. How can you accept and love yourself? With time, patience, affirmations, and forgiveness, you can begin to allow yourself to want something and know that you deserve it. If you are not self-accepting in your personal life, you will have trouble being self-accepting in your athletic life. And if you are living a life where your only identity is as an athlete or a sports star, when you are finished with your career, there is no self to be. You are lost.

You can have exactly what you want in your life, just as you can get what you want as an athlete. In life, as in athletics, the drive to achieve, to be all you can be, must come from within. It must be your choice. But first you must know what you want in life. This is a very difficult task, especially since people's wants and needs seem to change like the seasons. Also, the changes people want to make often seem so huge and overwhelming that they get frustrated before they take even the first step. Therefore, it is most important to be, think, and feel in the moment, right now. What do you want in life right now, today, this week?

At this point, using a mental training program for your life may seem more difficult than using one only for athletics. And this is true. Many times athletic wants and desires are much clearer. The vision of your athletic goals appears more tangible. "I want to run my first marathon." "I want to swim in open-water competition." These desires are straightforward and clear. But when it comes to desires in life, other emotions, other belief systems, and other people's opinions, requests, and expectations come into play. People become afraid to be honest, afraid to commit, and afraid to go against what they think they should want. These are common stumbling blocks; they are not right or wrong. They can be handled and they can be overcome. You really can have what you want in life because you have sole responsibility for what you get in life. As said earlier, the choice is always yours alone.

What you want can be more of what you already have, or it can be something different. It can seem impossible or quite easy. You must be honest and true to yourself. Allow yourself to want anything you want and back this up with affirmations such as the following:

I accept myself and others for who we are.

I am an open-minded and accepting person.

I forgive myself and others.

I deserve my dreams and wishes.

I am loveable and acceptable the way I am.

I love and accept others the way they are.

I give to myself and others the love and respect we all deserve.

I am different and that is wonderful.

I accept myself unconditionally.

I accept others unconditionally.

I love and respect myself.

When you are ready to really think about what you want in life, use Mental Trainer #12 to write these wants down just as they come. Put aside your fear of judgment, fear of failure, and fear of rejection. Just think of everything you have ever wanted to be, to do, or to have. Write it down. As you write, imagine yourself being, doing, and having exactly what you want. Feel how it feels to set yourself free in this way. Notice if there is any inner talk. Is it positive or negative or perhaps both? Set your mind free and allow yourself everything.

That feels very good, doesn't it? Does it feel a little frightening too? What if you actually got everything you wanted? Take a moment again to see yourself being what you have always wanted to be, doing what you have always wanted to do, and having what you have always wanted to have.

Now begin to rank your desires in the order of their greatest importance to you. Assume for this moment that you can have it all. Decide which ones are the most important and number

Mental Trainer #12:   What I Want

What I have always wanted in

- Life:

- Family:

- Friends:

- Myself:

them. You are in no hurry. Think this over as clearly as possible, realizing that wants sometimes change from day to day. Give yourself permission to be flexible. Your list might look something like this:

1. To be thin
2. To be well educated
3. To be prosperous
4. To own my own business
5. To have children

Now that you have a tangible idea of what you want in life, write down, starting with your most important wish, all the reasons why you can't have what you desire. Using Mental Trainer #13, do this for the four desires you want the most. This will help you clarify what you consider your limits and will help you to understand what keeps you from having what you really want in life.

Mental Trainer #13:   Roadblocks

1. Why I can't have what I want in life:

2. Why I can't have what I want in life:

3. Why I can't have what I want in life:

4. Why I can't have what I want in life:

(continued)

5. How I can overcome these roadblocks (action plan):

a.

b.

c.

d.

Visualization for Self-Acceptance

Think of a time when you felt . . . respected, accepted, understood, appreciated, or acknowledged . . . re-create that state
of mind and state of being . . . the sights, the sounds, the feelings . . . go back and remember it all . . . if you can't think of a
time, think of a person you know who is highly respected and
appreciated, and imagine being that person . . . experiencing
being respected, accepted, understood . . . and also remember
a time when you gave that to someone else . . . remembering
the feelings in your body as you gave that acknowledgment to
another person . . . and begin to think of a word that represents
these states of mind and states of being . . . knowing you are
capable of both giving and receiving these types of self-acceptance . . . giving it to others and deserving and receiving
it for yourself . . . know that it is possible to do both . . . and
that you and others are truly capable of creating a world and
environment where this is true . . . allowing yourself to see
that world . . . hear it . . . and feel it . . . say your affirmations
to yourself . . . the affirmations of respect, acceptance, appre-

ciation, friendship, support, and valuing others . . . and know that in time you will create these things in any situation that you are in . . . by practicing your own values of compassion and acceptance of yourself and others . . .

Say your word to yourself, experiencing in your body the feelings of whatever value you have picked today to create . . . allowing it to fill you with peace, harmony, and patience . . . knowing that you are helping create a new world of acceptance, tolerance, and peace . . .

Slowly let the images fade, coming back to your body sitting in the chair, or lying down . . . take a deep breath . . . remembering your word . . . and counting to three, open your eyes when you're ready . . . one . . . stretch your arms and legs . . . two . . . take a deep breath . . . stretching your neck and shoulders . . . and three . . . open your eyes.

Putting a Program Together

From these last two worksheets, you now have the material to begin the program defined in the first part of this book—that is, goal setting, affirmations, relaxation, visualization, and mental log keeping.

Take your four most important wants and form four goals. Focus specifically on what you want and the results you want to achieve. Be sure they are clear to you and that you know exactly what these goals mean to you and the results you really want. Here's an example: "I want to be prosperous. This means to feel secure; to have enough money to feel free; to have a job I love doing; to be healthy and well accepted in my group of friends and workplace." You may need to form steps or minigoals as described in chapter 4 to feel able to reach these goals and avoid feeling overwhelmed, frustrated, or afraid to start.

For every "but" or reason why you cannot do, be, or have something, there is an affirmation that will help you turn this reason around, to see the fallacy of it, and to let it go. Remember that a positive self-statement is present tense, positive, and personal, and it may not be exactly true at the moment. Therefore, "I don't have enough education" becomes "I am intelligent and capable"; "My mate would feel threatened" becomes "My mate listens and supports me, knowing that I care about him/her and his/her concerns." With every affirmation and positive visualization you use, you change old belief systems. You also form new ones that allow you to move and change, to achieve, to become, to do, and to have what you want. And of course, the more you get out of your life, the more you have to give to yourself, to those you care about, and to the world in general.

Take with you your most important goal and find a quiet spot. Slowly bring yourself through the goal achievement visualization in chapter 6 and begin to visualize yourself attaining this important goal. Remember to use all of your senses. See yourself succeeding, hear the support and enthusiasm from yourself and others, and feel the fullness of your heart and how it feels to accomplish this important desire. See, feel, and hear it all from the beginning to the end. Notice how simple it can be. Step-by-step, you move toward your goal until you triumph. Allow yourself to experience it all. You can create your own visualization exactly as you want it to be. You are always in control, and it is positive and good.

Do this for each goal, one at a time, saying your affirmations as you watch yourself succeed. If you have a small tape recorder, you can record your visualization and then listen to it any time you have a few minutes of quiet. Before you go to bed at night or in the morning upon awakening are usually good times. Anywhere it is peaceful and you are relaxed is a good place to do your visualization.

As your wants and desires change, and as you achieve your life goals, new ones will take their place. Keeping a mental training log for life goals will help you remember and focus on these new goals as they occur to you.

If you are willing to risk and to be dedicated to your mental training in your athletic endeavors, you will achieve your goals and eventually your peak performance. This is also true in life. The process is the same. Each new outcome, setback, and move forward is a learning experience and growth step. With each experience, each step, you go beyond your self-imposed limitations. You let go of your fear just a little and become willing to risk the next step.

Taking the Program With You

Successful people, successful leaders, and successful athletes have the following in common: they have a total belief in themselves

Marion Jones, Olympic gold medalist sprinter, has some of the best focusing techniques in the track world.

© Corbis

and their abilities; they have absolute and total concentration and focus; they do visualization or imagery of their performance for days or weeks before an event; they analyze any losses in order to improve performance, techniques, and strategy; they have the ability to let go of losses and failures easily and look forward to new challenges in future events; and they never see themselves as losers, even after losing a competition or experiencing failure. Successful people see failures as feedback, and they see losses as opportunities to do something different.

Top athletes are admired and looked up to as role models for all ages. As an athlete, think about what characteristics you have or would like to cultivate in yourself as a leader and role model for others. How do you want to live in the world and with what values? Integrity, accountability, respect, knowledge, wisdom, compassion, and self-knowledge are all values worthy of embody-ing and pursuing. All of these values come down to taking stock of yourself, what you believe in, and what kind of world you want to create for yourself, your family, your friends, your community, your country, and the world. Even though you are just one person, your actions, thoughts, and attitudes can make a difference in the world. It is the many "I's" that make up the "we." Use the What Are My Highest Values? worksheet to determine your values and how to go about cultivating them in yourself.

It is up to you to change the world into a more peaceful and lov-ing place for your children to inherit. It is your own learning and modeling of forgiveness, understanding, tolerance, compassion, and love that teaches your children the same values.

The intolerance of cheating or other questionable ethics helps to teach others the values of respect for self, others, and even personal property. An open, friendly attitude opens doors in any culture. And this comes from an openhearted, people-liking at-titude toward life in general. Indeed, your thoughts do create the reality that you live in. With positive thoughts and actions, you can create a more positive world. It's up to you.

Take a few minutes to think about your own values and habits. What values and habits serve you and which do not? The purpose of finding your values is so that you can consciously practice and embody them in your life. Life is full of conscious choices.

What Are My Highest Values?

1. **Value:** _____

    What actions can I take to live this value in my athletic life?

    a.

    b.

    c.

    What actions can I take to live this value in my personal life?

    a.

    b.

    c.

2. **Value:** _____

What actions can I take to live this value in my athletic life?

a.

b.

c.

What actions can I take to live this value in my personal life?

a.

b.

c.

3. **Value:** _____

What actions can I take to live this value in my athletic life?

a.

b.

c.

What actions can I take to live this value in my personal life?

a.

b.

c.

4. **Value:** _____

What actions can I take to live this value in my athletic life?

a.

b.

c.

What actions can I take to live this value in my personal life?

a.

b.

c.

Sit down with paper and pencil or at your computer and write a page about what kind of life you would like to live. Write it in the present tense as if it is already a reality. This is a form of writing down your intentions. Date it, sign it, and put it in a safe place. Read it one year from today. This is a good exercise to do on your birthday as a way of focusing on what you want to create in the future.

Another exercise to do at the end of each year or on your birthday is to write down all you have accomplished in the past year. The My Year in Review worksheet can help you with this. What are you grateful for in your life? Make a list of these things too. They may be small or large things such as your family, your dog, your friends, your warm home, your coach, your team, and so forth. Take a few minutes to focus on what is right and good in your life.

As you go forward and expand your mind and spirit in the 21st century, and begin to create more passion in your everyday life, here are a few helpful things to keep in mind:

My Year in Review

My accomplishments this past year:

Athletics   Personal life   Work/career   Other

What I am grateful for:

Athletics   Personal life   Work/career   Other

- Things in business or creative life actually expand as you cut back or limit your efforts.

- You are rewarded more as you let go and relax your efforts than when you strive to get something or when you exploit or force an issue.

- You prosper enormously when giving to or helping others and when forgetting about your own interests.

- Over time, enormous benefits come to you and to others from what you felt at first was a selfish act—something you did for yourself.

- Lasting lessons or some true good comes from the very problem or outcome you initially fear or find most painful.

- Small "deaths" or soul-wrenching losses open you up to a larger, fuller, richer life.

- Out of failures, mistakes, or unhappy events, you find opportunities for growth or find precepts that you then productively apply to other areas of your life.

The 21st century will require you to use your mind and spirit in far different ways than you have in the past. Embracing paradox will be important to you in prospering and living a life of mental, physical, and spiritual abundance and flexibility. Here is a visualization to help you increase your passion and vitality in life.

Visualization for Passion and Vitality

Begin to imagine and remember a time in the past when you felt good physically . . . strong, vibrant, enjoying life, and excited to be alive . . . if you can't think of a time, think of the healthiest and most vibrant person you know and imagine being them . . . in thinking of this time of aliveness, see the people you were with, the scene, the environment . . . all the colors; hear the sounds . . . and begin to feel the energy coursing through your body . . . that vitality, aliveness . . . feel yourself flowing with good health and energy . . . your heart pumping strongly . . . the blood flowing powerfully through your veins and arteries . . . your lungs drawing deep breaths of clear, clean, fresh air . . . feeling energized and full of good health . . .

Imagine yourself as you were then, perhaps a younger you . . . experience yourself as that vital, alive, vibrant, and healthy person . . . begin to notice that your head, face, and jaw are relaxing . . . they are softening, becoming limber and flexible . . . and feel them to be energized at the same time . . . notice that your shoulders, back, and neck are relaxed, supple, and flexible . . . recall all those feelings of health, strength, power, and vitality . . . all those feelings, sounds, and images . . . feel them coursing through your body . . . from head, neck, shoulders, and back, through your chest, stomach, and abdomen . . . feel the energy and strength going down into the rest of your body . . . into your upper arms, elbows, lower arms, and hands . . . into your thighs, knees, and calves, down into your feet . . . feeling the aliveness and alertness . . . and the healthy red blood cells in your veins and arteries . . . bringing oxygen to every part of your body . . .

Experience how this vitality feels and sounds . . . and think of the words *vibrant* and *alive* . . . say those words over to yourself . . . associating those words with this healthy and vital state of mind and being . . . say the words to yourself in your mind . . . and feel those feelings in your body . . . a reminder of a time of peak energy, vitality, and health . . . being and feeling energetic, healthy, and strong . . .

Begin to notice that you are feeling more relaxed, alert, interested, and excited about this new vitality and awareness in your body . . . notice that you are feeling those feelings in your body right now . . . know that you can remember and bring into your body those feelings, sensations, sounds, and visions any time you wish . . . merely by relaxing and letting your mind drift back to that healthy and youthful state . . . deeply breathe fresh air into your lungs, relax your neck and shoulders . . . and say the words to yourself, "vibrant and alive," bringing back all those sounds, images, and feelings . . . remember that you have within you everything that you need to re-create that experience . . . enjoy that state, live it, breathe it; vitalize and celebrate your body . . .

When you are ready, begin to let go of those images, saying the words to yourself slowly . . . take a deep breath, let it go with a sigh . . . slowly coming back to your body sitting in the chair or lying down . . . take another deep breath, and let it out, relaxing your chest, upper back, and neck . . . when you are ready, you may open your eyes, feeling awake, alert, relaxed, healthy, and vital . . . ready for the rest of your day.

Becoming the Best You Can Be

This book has suggested to you many ways of achieving your potential and improving your mental training skills. Completing the Mental Trainer worksheets will help you see your strengths and weaknesses and will point you in the direction of your best performances. I have often thought of *The Mental Athlete* as the first step to profound mental consciousness for athletes. The processes in this book help you think about how you perform mentally and psychologically. If you practice these methods, you will find yourself enjoying your sport even more. I *know* you can do it; it's just a matter of you having the same discipline in your mental practice as you have in your physical practice.

All these internal musings and contemplations will help you to become more balanced in mind, body, spirit, and emotions. With this balance in your life, you can become a positive contributor in a world that is in desperate need of positive contributions. Now is the time, you are the person. If not you, then who? Be committed to your life and remember that you count and you can make a difference.

I once facilitated a group that in my opinion was a total disaster. It was chaotic, it didn't flow, and the members were contentious and argumentative. Nothing went right, and I felt I had failed miserably as a leader in my facilitation. Three years later, one of the participants came up to me and said, "What you said in that group changed my life." I was stunned. I no longer remember what it was that I said, but my lesson from that event was that even when you think you have failed or haven't contributed to someone's learning, you most likely have at some level, in at least one person's life.

In teaching and coaching, I see myself as putting something valuable on the table for the athletes to take. It is up to them to pick it up and take it. I try to make it appealing and useful. So it is with this book. There are entrees, vegetables, and fruits along with desserts and snacks. Pick up what appeals to you and let it nourish your body and soul. Leave behind what you don't want for others. And always remember to savor the experience in the moment. For the moment is all you really have because the past is gone and the future isn't here yet. Bon appétit!

Be present,
Be aware,
Be awake . . .
Honor your individual spirit,
your individual freedom,
your individual responsibility.
Honor your part in the greater whole,
your part in the greater universe . . .
Be true to yourself,
Believe in yourself.
Know in your heart
what is right for you.
Say yes to your dreams . . .

References

Andrisani, J. 2002. *Think Like Tiger.* New York, NY: G. P. Putnam.

Bardwick, J. and E. Douvan. 1972. Ambivalence: The socialization of women. In J. Bardwick (Ed.), *Readings on the psychology of women.* New York: Harper & Row.

Brown, J. 2001. *Sports Talent.* Champaign, IL: Human Kinetics.

Clark, N. 1997. *Nancy Clark's Sports Nutrition Guidebook.* Champaign, IL: Human Kinetics.

Clark, N. 2002. *The Food Guide For Marathoners.* West Newton, MA: Sports Nutrition Publishers.

Garfield, C. 1984. *Peak Performance.* Los Angeles, CA: J. P. Tarcher.

Goldberg, A. 1998. *Sports Slump Busting.* Champaign, IL: Human Kinetics.

Goldberg, A. 1998. Breaking Out of a Slump. *Penn State Sports Medicine Newsletter* 6, no.10 (June).

Harris, D. and B. Harris. 1984. *An Athlete's Guide to Sports Psychology.* Champaign, IL: Human Kinetics.

Houston, J. 1997. *The Possible Human.* Los Angeles, CA: J. P. Tarcher.

Jackson, P. 1995. *Sacred Hoops: Spiritual Lessons of a Hardwood Warrior.* New York: Hyperion.

Jeffers, S. 1988. *Feel the Fear and Do It Anyway.* New York, NY: Ballantine Books.

Kubler-Ross, E. 1997. *On Death and Dying.* Garden City, NY: Anchor Press.

Levine, S. 1987. *Healing Into Life and Death.* Garden City, NY: Anchor Press.

Levine, S. 1991. *Guided Meditations, Explorations and Healings.* Garden City, NY: Anchor Press.

Loehr, J. and T. Gullikson. 2002. Maintaining Technique Under Pressure. *Georgia Tech Sports Medicine & Performance Newsletter* 10, no. 6 (March): 2.

Matthews-Simonton, S., O.C. Simonton, and J.L. Creighton. 1978. *Getting Well Again.* Los Angeles, CA: J. P. Tarcher.

Murphy, S. 1995. *Sport Psychology Interventions.* Champaign, IL: Human Kinetics.

Northrup, C. 2002. Cannabis Abuse and the Brain. *Health Wisdom for Women* 9, no. 9 (September).

Pipher, M. 2002. *Reviving Ophelia.* New York, NY: Ballantine Books.

RGN News Service Reports, "Eugene Prep Sets State Shotput Mark," *Eugene Register Guard,* 27 April 1997.

Roetert, P. and J. Groppel. 2001. *World Class Tennis Technique.* Champaign, IL: Human Kinetics.

Rotella, R. and S. Heyman. 1993. Stress Imagery and the Psychological Rehabilitation of Athletes. In J. Williams, *Applied Sport Psychology,* Second Edition. Mountainview, CA: Mayfield Publishing.

Roth, G. 1991. *When Food Is Love.* New York, NY: Macmillan.

Swoap, R.A. and S. Murphy. 1995. Eating disorders and weight management in athletes. In S. Murphy (Ed.), *Sport Psychology Interventions.* Champaign, IL: Human Kinetics.

Ungerleider, S. 2001. *Faust's Gold: Inside the East German Doping Machine.* New York, NY: St. Martin's Press.

Wilstein, S., "New Martina on Top Again Down Under," *Eugene Register Guard,* 31 January 1998.

Zang, F. *The Olympian,* February-March 1997.

Index

Note: The italicized *f* and *t* following page numbers refer to figures and tables, respectively.

About the Author

© Rosanne Olson

Kay Porter, PhD, has worked in the sport psychology field since 1979 and has trained hundreds of athletes and teams. She is the owner of Porter Performance Systems, a training, counseling, and consulting company. Formerly a professor at the University of Oregon, she spent 13 years as a sport psychology consultant to the athletic department.

She is a member of the U.S. Olympic Committee Sport Psychology Registry and a consultant in sport psychology, certified by the Association for the Advancement of Applied Sport Psychology (AAASP). She is considered an international expert in the field of mental training and has given presentations and workshops at conferences nationally and internationally.

Porter is a former varsity athlete in tennis and was a national champion in master's track in the 1500 meters and competed in master's running for 20 years. Additionally, she coaches a walking group every year for the Portland Marathon. Porter has published more than 30 articles on mental training and peak performance and has produced two videotapes and 20 recorded guided visualizations for sports performance. She wrote *The Mental Athlete* in its original version and was published in English, German, French, and Japanese. Additionally, she is the author of a book titled *Visual Athletics* published by W.C. Brown/McGraw-Hill.

Porter lives in Eugene, Oregon, and enjoys running and walking marathons, hiking, meditating, and traveling. For more information on Kay Porter visit www.thementalathlete.com.

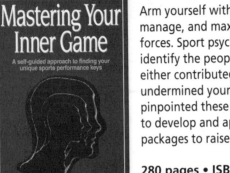